NASCAR ESSENTIAL

Everything You Need to Know to Be a Real Fan!

David Poole and Jim McLaurin

TRIUMPH
BOOKS

Library of Congress Cataloging-in-Publication Data

Poole, David, 1959–
    NASCAR essential : everything you need to know to be a real fan!
/ David Poole and Jim McLaurin.
        p. cm.
    ISBN-13: 978-1-57243-955-9 (hardcover)
    ISBN-10: 1-57243-955-6 (hardcover)
        1. NASCAR (Association)—History. 2. Stock car racing—United
    States—History.   I. McLaurin, James, 1946– II. Title.

GV1029.9.S74P64 2007
796.72—dc22

                                                    2006033611

This book is available in quantity at special discounts for your group or organization. For further information, contact:

Triumph Books
542 South Dearborn Street
Suite 750
Chicago, Illinois 60605
(312) 939-3330
Fax (312) 663-3557

Printed in U.S.A.
ISBN: 978-1-57243-955-9
Design by Patricia Frey
All photos courtesy of AP/Wide World Photos except where otherwise indicated

To all those who helped pave the road to success that NASCAR runs on today.

Contents

Acknowledgments vii

Introduction by David Poole ix

Still Climbing the Ladder 1

Vive la Frances 8

A Champ Named Red as NASCAR Takes the Green 15

Absolutely Fabulous 19

Racing's Royal Family 24

A Pair but Not Two of a Kind 31

Win until You're Done 37

Wizards with Wrenches 43

Dreamers and Doers 48

Second to None 54

Smoke and Dollars 60

Buck and Buddy 64

Triumph and Tragedy 69

Checks, Credit, and Cash 78

Fare Thee Well, BP 85

Cale's Long, Hard Fight 89

Keeping the Jaws Working 93

EARN-HARDT! 98

Boys Will Be Boys 104

Thrills, Spills, and Dollar Bills—All-Star Style 113

Million Dollar Bill 119

Promise Unfulfilled 124

Two's Company, Three's a Crowd, and Four's a Team 132

A Clean Break 139

Brother to Brother 144

Making His Mark 149

Perfect? No—But Still a Wonder 154

His Own Dale 160

Discovering Columbus 167

Who's Next? 174

Answers to Trivia Questions 180

Appendix A: NASCAR Tracks 182

Appendix B: All-Time NASCAR Cup Champions 190

All-Time Nextel Cup Driver List 193

Acknowledgments

One by-product of NASCAR's growing popularity has been the opportunity for people like us to do books like this, telling some of the sport's rich and colorful history. But NASCAR historian Greg Fielden was doing that long before it became trendy. Without his definitive volumes and the exhaustive research behind them, much of the sport's history might be lost in the collective fog of failing memories.

Similarly, the sport is richer today because a handful of people have made the effort to chart its statistical history. Len Thacher and Michael Payne, the two key men behind NASCAR Statistical Services, have kept NASCAR beat writers straight on the sport's records for so long they are sometimes taken for granted, and that's a shame.

Many of the charts and lists in this book also credit www.racing-reference.info as the source of statistical data. Alan Boodman of Monroeville, Pennsylvania, operates that site on his own simply because he has both the interest and the expertise to do it.

Boodman will tell you that when he started assembling the database that drives his site, he went to Greg Fielden's Forty Years of Stock Car Racing series of history books and used the race reports listed there to provide the data.

So, in some ways, it all gets back to Fielden. Hey, Greg, we owe you dinner.

—David Poole and Jim McLaurin

Acknowledgments

Introduction

In trying to be true to the title of this book, Jim McLaurin and I began this project by attempting to come up with a list of people whose careers and contributions have been essential to NASCAR's growth and success.

Two problems become immediately apparent when you try that.

First, you just have to accept the fact that you'll never, ever get to cover everybody who deserves to be singled out and have his or her story told. Heck, the great mechanic Smokey Yunick wrote a three-volume set on his own life alone, and we could only find about half a chapter for him in here.

Second, you have to realize that a certain amount of overlap is absolutely unavoidable. You can't, for instance, talk about the fight at the end of the 1979 Daytona 500 only in the story about Cale Yarborough or only in the chapter about the Allison clan. History is like a tote bag full of tangled earplugs and computer cords and cell phone chargers that are almost impossible to pull apart. So if you find yourself with a sense of déjà vu as you work through these pages, relax. It's not your mind that's slipping.

This book is not a comprehensive history of NASCAR. It is rather an anecdotal outline of some of the highlights, told in terms of the key moments and key players who were there for them. If you have been a race fan your whole life, we hope you will still learn a few things and that we managed to drum up a few nice memories along the way. If you're fairly new to the sport, maybe we'll help you get a grasp on just how far things have come and how much fun people have had along the way.

—David Poole

Still Climbing the Ladder

On his way to the 2005 Nextel Cup championship, Tony Stewart found a different way to celebrate victories in NASCAR's top series.

After wining at Daytona International Speedway in July, Stewart parked his car at the start/finish line of the massive 2.5-mile racetrack. A former Indy Racing League champion who left open-wheel racing to take part in what has become—by a huge margin—America's most popular motorsports series, Stewart climbed from his No. 20 Chevrolet, ran to the fence between the track and its massive grandstands, and began climbing.

Stewart would admit later that he underestimated how difficult it would be to get over the outward curve at the top of that 20-foot-tall fence. But he made it and stood in the flag stand with the checkered flag, celebrating with his fans.

It was an electric moment.

It also turned out to be a marketing opportunity.

Stewart's NASCAR team, owned by Joe Gibbs, is sponsored by The Home Depot. During the week after that race, the company placed full-page ads in several newspapers around the country showing a picture of Stewart trying to get to the top of that fence.

"Hey Tony," the ad read. "We have ladders." The Home Depot offered customers who brought the ad in a discount on the purchase of ladders, and sales rose by a double-digit percentage in the immediate aftermath.

It's hard to come up with a better example of how NASCAR—the National Association for Stock Car Auto Racing—has grown from a regional curiosity into a national sports phenomenon.

Tony Stewart celebrates winning the Pepsi 400 in his traditional fashion, by climbing the fence and waving to fans.

Auto racing has been a part of the American sports culture for the better part of a century. There were races at Indianapolis Motor Speedway before World War I, and cars ran on tracks made of lumber carried from town to town in boxcars at various places around the country before the Great Depression.

But the idea of racing "stock" cars—literally taking cars off an auto dealer's showroom floor and racing them after only taping up the headlights, yanking off the hubcaps, rigging some rudimentary form of seat belt system, and painting or taping a number on the door—wasn't born until after World War II.

It took a while for things to get organized, but once there was such a thing as NASCAR the seeds of what's happening today were planted. Cars raced at Martinsville Speedway in Virginia, in the first season of what is now called the Nextel Cup Series, in 1949. And although the track was red dirt then and is a mixture of asphalt and concrete today, the series still races there.

In South Carolina, Darlington Raceway, stock car racing's first true superspeedway, came online the next year. Throughout the 1950s, the sport put down its roots and developed a loyal following. By 1960, Daytona was already up and running—and running fast, too—while major tracks in Charlotte and Atlanta were being completed.

In 1960, the average race in what was then called the Grand National Series paid a total purse of $13,601. The largest total purse was $78,980 and the sport's national champion, Rex White, took home $57,525 for the year.

A decade later, Bobby Isaac was champion and he won $199,600. It wasn't until 1985 that any one race paid a total purse of more than $1 million. That was the Daytona 500, and until 1994 it was still the only race that had ever listed a total purse in seven figures.

But things were changing.

In the early 1970s, R.J. Reynolds Tobacco Company became the title sponsor of the sport's top series. That relationship would endure for more than 30 years, and RJR helped NASCAR financially and with promotional assistance that soon began to pay off.

There had been some early interest in NASCAR from television networks, mainly in the form of ABC airing taped portions of races on its legendary *Wide World of Sports* series. But when CBS decided

TOP 5

Seating Capacities for NASCAR Nextel Cup Tracks

Indianapolis Motor Speedway	280,000
Daytona International Speedway	168,000
Lowe's Motor Speedway	165,000
Bristol Motor Speedway	160,000
Texas Motor Speedway	159,585

Source: 2006 NASCAR Media Guide

to air the Daytona 500 live, from flag to flag, in 1979, the sport got an opportunity to show its stuff.

After that watershed event, television fell in love with NASCAR in the 1980s. One particularly ardent partner was a then-fledgling cable network known as ESPN. Hungry for programming, ESPN started taking on the challenge of airing live races and found a national audience. By the mid-1990s, every Winston Cup race was being shown live on one of several networks spread across the dial. The national media began to notice that something was going on in NASCAR.

Richard Petty's 200 career victories had been enough to make his nickname—the King—known far and wide. Then, a driver from a small textile-mill town in North Carolina called Kannapolis came along and Dale Earnhardt challenged Petty's record of seven championships. About the same time, race fans were first being introduced to an impossibly young kid from Indiana named Jeff Gordon.

Suddenly, NASCAR was booming. Gleaming new facilities, some of the largest and most elaborate sports facilities in the country, were being built near cities like Los Angeles, Dallas–Fort Worth, Chicago, and Las Vegas. Existing tracks were adding seats as fast as people who build grandstands could get them assembled.

In the sport's early years, drivers would agree to paint the name of a local repair shop or car dealer on their cars and get a few dollars or maybe some spare parts in return. When Petty was reigning over the sport, he became synonymous with STP, a brand of oil additive, and in that era almost every other sponsor in the sport was related to automobiles, beer, and tobacco.

But through the 1990s, products like Tide detergent, McDonald's restaurants, and Kodak film bought into the NASCAR experience. What these companies found, to their delight, is that the sport's fans are not only loyal to their favorite driver and the kind of car he or she drives, but also to the product that sponsors the car.

When Earnhardt's son, Dale Earnhardt Jr., signed his first sponsorship deal with Budweiser in 1999, it was reportedly worth $8 million per year. How in the world, asked some of the people who'd

By the NUMBERS

How NASCAR Race Purses Have Grown

Year	Largest purse	Races	Total purse	Avg. purse
1960	$78,980	44	$598,434	$13,601
1970	$155,735	48	$2,017,657	$42,035
1980	$604,875	31	$5,400,870	$174,222
1990	$1,746,392	29	$14,664,462	$505,671
1995	$4,030,280	31	$32,307,944	$1,042,192
2001	$9,678,524	36	$116,968,224	$3,249,117
2005	$14,322,448	36	$179,644,707	$4,990,131

Source: www.racing-reference.info

been around for the sport's lean years, could anyone ever spend that much to field a NASCAR team?

Not long after that, NASCAR decided it was time to consolidate its television rights that, to that point, had been sold individually by each of the tracks that hosted Cup events. In 2000, the sport's total television revenue was around $100 million. When the first comprehensive network deal went into effect the next season, the six-year contract had an annual average of four times that.

In 2001, Gordon won his fourth career Cup title and took home $10,897,757.

In 1990, the total of the entire purses for all 29 races that year was $14,664,462. In 2006, the total purse for the Daytona 500—one race—was $18,029,052. Jimmie Johnson won $1,505,124 for his victory in that race.

For the past few years, about every six months another major national newspaper or magazine or television network "discovers" the NASCAR success story. Some people are still surprised when they learn that in any given year, 17 of the 20 largest crowds that assemble for a sporting event in this country do that to watch a Nextel Cup

TOP 10

Victory Leaders, All–Time and Modern Era*

All-Time	Modern Era (Since 1972)**
1. Richard Petty, 200	1. Darrell Waltrip, 84
2. David Pearson, 105	2. Dale Earnhardt, 76
3. Bobby Allison, 85	3. Jeff Gordon, 75
4. Darrell Waltrip, 84	4. Cale Yarborough, 69
5. Cale Yarborough, 83	5. Richard Petty, 60
6. Dale Earnhardt, 76	6. Bobby Allison, 55
7. Jeff Gordon, 75	Rusty Wallace, 55 †
8. Rusty Wallace, 55	8. David Pearson, 45
9. Lee Petty, 54	9. Bill Elliott, 44
10. Ned Jarrett, 50	10. Mark Martin, 35
Junior Johnson, 50 †	

* As of September 22, 2006.

**NASCAR's premier series began in 1949 with the first "strictly stock" race. In 1972, the series trimmed its schedule, eliminating dirt tracks and all tracks smaller than a half mile. Statistics beginning at that point are referred to as the sport's modern era.

Source: NASCAR Statistical Services

race. Some people are still surprised to find out that the sale of NASCAR-related merchandise and apparel has become nearly a $1 billion business each year.

Race fans, as far back as 1949 when the first race was held in Charlotte, North Carolina, have known all along their sport is something special. The crowd that day was bigger than anyone ever expected, and NASCAR has been surprising people ever since.

In 2004 NASCAR revised the system by which it picks its champion each year. The basic system by which drivers accumulate points for their finish in each race hasn't changed much since the early years of Winston's involvement. Each finishing position is assigned a point value, descending from first to last. Drivers also can get bonus points for leading laps in each race. Until 2004, points scored in all 36 races were added up and the driver with the most points at season's end was named the champion.

That changed when NASCAR introduced the Chase for the Nextel Cup, which divides the season into two parts. Now, the 10 drivers who score the most points in the first 26 races qualify for the Chase. Before the 27th race, the points totals for these drivers are reset so that only five points separates each position. Then, they spend the season's final 10 races trying to accumulate enough points to win the championship.

Stewart did that last year, winning his second career title in NASCAR. He got to the top of the Nextel Cup ladder and collected $13,578,168.

Remember that $8 million sponsorship deal for Earnhardt Jr.? In 2007, a team getting $8 million from a primary sponsor is still looking for another sponsor to pay for the other half of the season if it wants to keep up with the racing Joneses.

New television deals with Fox, TNT, Speed, and ABC/ESPN will bring in an estimated $4.5 billion over the next eight years. In a world where viewership has become increasingly fragmented, NASCAR's television audiences enjoyed dramatic growth over the term of the previous television deal.

Any way you look at it, the ladder just keeps getting taller.—D.P.

Vive la Frances

It's funny how often the right people seem to wind up in the right place.

Take, for example, William Henry Getty France Sr. In 1935, he was heading south from Washington, D.C., to Miami, looking for a warmer place to open a gas station and garage and to live with his wife and two-year-old son, Bill Jr.

The Frances didn't make it to Miami. Their car made it to Florida all right, but it broke down well up the coast in the city of Daytona Beach.

Close enough, France decided.

He opened his filling station on Main Street, just a few blocks from an archway through which, three decades earlier, young daredevils passed in their automobiles to take to the beach to try to set land speed records on the flat, wide sands. Speed had always meant dollars to Daytona, but when cars started going so fast that the speed trials moved to somewhere more wide open—the Bonneville Salt Flats in Utah—the Florida community had to come up with something of their own.

They came up with the idea to stage races on a course that ran partly on the beach and partly on the highway fronting it. The city and a local civic club both tried to run the events but were about to give up when they turned to the man whose garage had become a place where local car enthusiasts congregated.

France took on the challenge of promoting the 1938 beach and road race, and thousands of people showed up to watch. France managed to show a $200 profit at the end of the day.

Close your eyes and imagine that $200. A small pile of wrinkled $1 and $5 bills left over after all the bills had been paid.

DID YOU KNOW ... The France family's influence on NASCAR is bigger than Brian France, the current chairman and chief executive officer? Jim France, Brian's uncle and the brother of former NASCAR president Bill France Jr., is chief executive officer of International Speedway Corporation. Lesa France Kennedy, Brian's sister and Bill Jr.'s daughter, is president of that company, which owns and operates racetracks such as Daytona International Speedway, Darlington Raceway, Talladega Superspeedway, and several others around the country. Jim France and Lesa France Kennedy also are members of the NASCAR board of directors.

Now, imagine the Daytona International Speedway of today, filled with nearly 175,000 fans for the Daytona 500, NASCAR's premier event. Some individual seats in the track's massive grandstands sell for $200 or more—each.

Imagine the billions of dollars now involved in a sport that draws millions of fans to huge modern speedways from coast to coast piled up in that same fashion as that $200 profit in 1938.

It boggles the mind.

So does the enduring presence of the France family, which has been a constant from those humble beginnings right up until today when Brian France, the third generation leader of a sport his grandfather helped bring to life and his father, Bill Jr., helped build into an empire.

Racing didn't begin with the beach-and-road race in Daytona. As long as there had been cars, there had been men who tried to make them go fast. Ray Harroun won the first Indianapolis 500 in 1911, and in Appalachia, moonshiners, who carried illegal whiskey by night, competed against each other in their souped-up cars on county fairground tracks throughout the 1930s and 1940s.

When World War II ended, racing bounced back quickly. In the fall of 1945 France was in Charlotte, North Carolina, to promote a race on a dirt track at the fairgrounds there. He dropped in on Wilton Garrison, the sports editor of the *Charlotte Observer*, to try to get some publicity for the event.

"I told Wilton I was going to stage a national championship race out at the fairgrounds," France would later say. Garrison asked France

TRIVIA

Bill France Sr. was the promoter for the 1938 race on the beach and road course at Daytona. When the race was over the apparent winner of the race just kept on going and drove to a garage in Daytona Beach before later returning for postrace inspection. France, suspecting something fishy had gone on, disqualified the winner. Who was the victory awarded to?

Answers to the trivia questions are on pages 180–181.

who was going to race, and France listed some of the competitors.

"Wilton said, 'How can you call it a national championship race with local boys like that running?'" France said. "'Maybe you could call it a Southern championship, but there's no way it's a national championship race.'"

Garrison told France he needed a series of races with consistent rules and a championship points system, and suggested France get the American Automobile Association, which sanctioned the Indy car races, to sanction his series as well. But the AAA wasn't interested, and France wound up creating his own group.

France wasn't alone in trying to get stock-car racing wider respect, though, and in late 1947 he convened a meeting at the Streamline Hotel in Daytona Beach. It was at this meeting that the National Association for Stock Car Auto Racing (NASCAR) was born.

NASCAR ran a season's worth of races for modified cars in 1948, but it was in June 1949 at a three-quarter-mile dirt track near the airport in Charlotte where the sanctioning body held the first race in its Strictly Stock series—the forerunner of today's Nextel Cup Series.

France was NASCAR's first president, and after that first race in Charlotte he wound up with the kind of power that would serve him and the two generations that would follow in that same post well.

Glenn Dunnaway finished first in that inaugural event, but afterward it was discovered his car had illegal springs in the rear end. Dunnaway was disqualified and the victory given to Kansan Jim Roper. Hubert Westmoreland, Dunnaway's car owner, challenged the disqualification in court, but a judge ruled that NASCAR had the right to make and enforce its own rules.

From that point on, "Big Bill" France's word virtually became law in the sport. As he ruled with a stern hand, his son, Bill Jr., worked in just about every imaginable job in racing. At the first Southern 500 at Darlington Raceway in South Carolina, the younger France sold sno-cones. When he ran out of the flavoring to squirt on the shaved ice, he invented a new flavor—"plain"—and went right on selling. He also sold tickets to the beach race in Daytona.

"Tickets cost about $4," Bill France Jr. said. "I would start at the south end and work my way up to the north end, waking people up who were sleeping on the dunes. They either had to pay to watch the race or get off the course.

"As the crowds grew, we kept shortening the race. You had to get everybody in, run the race, and get everybody off before the tide

Former NASCAR president and current co–vice chairman, Bill France Jr., gives the command to "Start your engines" to kick off the 2005 racing season in Nashville, Tennessee.

DID YOU KNOW . . .

NASCAR founder William H.G. France was twice faced with the prospect of having the drivers in his sport form a union, and both times he shot it down? That's almost literally what happened the first time. In 1961, Curtis Turner was leading an effort to have the Teamsters, who had loaned Turner money to help him complete construction of Charlotte Motor Speedway, organize drivers. In August, France came to a race in Winston-Salem and told the competitors that no known union member could drive in NASCAR, saying he'd be more than happy to use the pistol he carried to enforce that. Before having a union forced on him, France threatened to shut NASCAR down, "plow it up, and plant corn."

The unionization effort failed and France banned Turner and Tim Flock, who had signed on to help Turner, from the sport for several years.

In 1969, France was opening the new track he'd built near Talladega, Alabama. The massive 2.66-mile speedway was clearly going to be the fastest track that NASCAR had ever run on, and after Charlie Glotzbach won the pole at 199.466 mph, tire companies were worried their products couldn't hold up to the forces being placed on them by the high speeds.

The recently formed Professional Drivers Association, led by Richard Petty, decided to take a stand. Without safe tires, the race should be called off, the PDA said. France disagreed, and to show he was right he strapped on a driver's helmet and borrowed a car. He went out and ran laps at a considerably slower speed, but contended that if he could do it so could the sport's top stars.

The PDA would not relent, and the afternoon before the race many of its members packed up and left the track. France, determined that the show would go on, recruited drivers from a support series and anywhere else he could find them and staged the Talladega 500 as scheduled the next day. Richard Brickhouse was the race winner.

Drivers in the PDA saw that France would run his events with or without them. That broke the back of the association, which disbanded within a couple of years.

came back in again. The more people you had, the longer it took to get them in and get them off. You either had to shorten the race or stop selling tickets, and being a good capitalist, that didn't make any sense."

Bill Jr. was a flagman, a scorer, a race steward, and even a driver. A photo showing Bill Jr. driving heavy machinery during the construction of Daytona International Speedway, which opened in 1959, is prominently displayed at NASCAR's headquarters. It is not a staged photo. Bill France Jr. spent months driving that machine and others like it to help his father's 2.5-mile dream of a track become a reality.

Bill Jr. learned at his father's side while serving as NASCAR vice president for six years.

"One of the key things I learned from him was evaluating the long-term benefit against the short-term negative and also the reverse," France Jr. said, "and then trying to rationalize whether you are better off to take the hit now because it makes sense tomorrow, or take the good today and worry when tomorrow comes."

The elder France turned over the NASCAR presidency to Bill Jr. in 1972 on the brink of a new era. R.J. Reynolds Tobacco Company, through its Winston brand of cigarettes, had signed on to sponsor the sport's top series a year earlier when tobacco advertising was banned from television.

What was later renamed the Winston Cup Series ran its last race on a dirt track in 1971 and, in 1972, streamlined its schedule to run only on tracks a half mile or longer. After running 48 races in 1971, the schedule was cut to 31 the following year and hasn't been higher than the current number of 36 events since.

For the first time in 1976, Winston Cup topped all other American racing series in attendance with 1.4 million fans, and it has remained at the top of that list. Current annual attendance in the Nextel Cup Series alone is estimated at more than 6 million. The sport has also emerged as a top-tier television product and has seen remarkable growth in its merchandising business and corporate sponsorships of its tracks and teams.

Richard Petty once described the differences between "Big Bill" and his son.

"You could talk to Senior all day long and then he'd do what he intended to do in the first place," Petty said. "Junior, you can talk to him and he'll listen to you. He'll talk to some other cats, too, and he'll weigh the pros and cons and then make his decision."

Bill France Sr. passed away in 1992. His son led NASCAR through nearly three decades of tremendous growth.

"We've just got to keep pushing the race cars up the hill," France Jr. said in describing his philosophy. "We have to keep the sport moving forward."

In 2000 France Jr. named Mike Helton NASCAR president. Helton is still the only person not named France to hold that title, but in 2002 it was Brian France, Bill Jr.'s son, who was named chairman of the board and chief executive officer of the sport.

Brian France has a background in marketing and has been credited with creating the sport's three-year-old "Chase for the Nextel Cup" championship format. He was instrumental in negotiating its first network television deal that began in 2001 and again had a leadership role in the second contract that starts in 2007.

"I don't think I should or can make every decision," Brian France said, speaking about how things have changed since his grandfather's reign. "There are a whole lot more decisions that need to be made. I can't make them all and I don't want to.

"We have 850 people working for NASCAR, and a lot of good people. One way to lose good people is if you don't let them make decisions and take a couple of chances. I couldn't if I wanted to micromanage the sport like we did way back when. It's too big for that. Even if I could, that wouldn't be smart."—D.P.

A Champ Named Red as NASCAR Takes the Green

Robert N. "Red" Byron was the first champion in NASCAR's Strictly Stock division in 1949, but he was a racer long before NASCAR came into being.

Byron was, in fact, NASCAR's first "crowned" champion, winning its modified championship in 1948, a year before the Strictly Stock division came into being. Indeed, he won the first NASCAR race (February 15, 1948) a week before NASCAR itself was incorporated.

Racing was around long before William H.G. France and his cronies hammered out a rudimentary set of rules by which they thought stock-car racing ought to live. Byron raced all through the 1930s and early 1940s, most notably in modified races on the beach-road course at Daytona Beach, Florida, that were promoted by France. Byron had the good fortune of hooking up with Georgia's Raymond Parks, stock-car racing's first big-time car owner, and Red Vogt, the best mechanic of that era.

Even as NASCAR got off the ground, not everyone was as convinced as France that the public was ready to see cars right off the showroom floor involved in the barely controlled mayhem that defined modified racing.

Modifieds, in essence, were jalopies, and nobody minded seeing them banging into each other. But particularly after World War II, when the country had gone five years without an automobile being built, new cars were still in short supply. In 1947 and 1948, the average Joe—who was still driving his beat-up 1940 Ford—didn't favor the idea of seeing someone tear up a brand-new car on a racetrack.

But it was France's contention that the American public would identify more closely with cars like the ones they could buy, and might perhaps let some of those barroom arguments about whose car was fastest be settled on a track by professionals instead of by half-drunk crazies on the nation's highways. (The jury's still out on that one.)

It was a noble idea, but in practice no car that's ever raced in NASCAR has been strictly stock. Before the first race at Charlotte on June 19, 1949, drivers were allowed to weld a plate onto the right front wheel of their cars in the interest of safety, to prevent the lug nuts from pulling through the rims on the stock wheels as they negotiated the turns.

It was not, however, permissible to alter cars the way that the 1947 Ford driven by Glenn Dunnaway was. The car, owned by Hubert Westmoreland, breezed across the finish line three laps ahead of Kansan Jim Roper's Lincoln. Major Al Crisler, NASCAR's first technical inspector, noted how effortlessly Dunnaway's car cruised through the turns and called for a postrace inspection.

It was discovered that the wheel springs did not fit the specifications, since the car Dunnaway drove was a bootlegger car that had been modified to carry heavy loads of moonshine by "spreading the springs." NASCAR disqualified Dunnaway and awarded the $2,000 first prize to Roper. Westmoreland filed a protest the only way he knew how, by suing NASCAR for $10,000.

Judge John J. Hayes threw the case out of a Greensboro, North Carolina, court, saying NASCAR had a right to enforce its own rules, and NASCAR was off and running. In the 21st century, much has changed, but the underlying premises of Big Bill's dream are intact. NASCAR may not always be right, but it rarely loses.

A few of the stocks ran with the modifieds in the 1948 season, but they were not plentiful enough to make a full division, much less fulfill France's vision of making Strictly Stock the premier class.

Which is why, in France's mind, Byron made an illogical inaugural champion. It was likely to Big Bill's everlasting chagrin, but Byron was not dedicated to the pure stocks. Even after his first win in one, Byron said he preferred the speedier modifieds.

Although Byron won two of the six Strictly Stock races he entered in 1949 (out of eight total races), those six would be the only races for which he got credit for entering.

TOP 10

Victory Leaders in NASCAR's Premier Series (1949–59)

Driver	Wins	Races	Top 5s	Poles	Earnings
1. Lee Petty	48	379	206	14	$203,705
Herb Thomas	48†	227	122	39	$139,433
3. Buck Baker	40	312	170	42	$166,126
4. Tim Flock	39	178	102	38	$107,500
5. Fireball Roberts	21	127	53	12	$88,502
6. Fonty Flock	19	153	72	33	$73,066
7. Speedy Thompson	18	182	74	19	$91,421
8. Junior Johnson	16	110	40	5	$39,236
Curtis Turner	16†	128	44	12	$60,215
10. Dick Rathman	13	128	69	13	$55,279

Source: www.racing-reference.info

The other winners in that inaugural season, by the way, were Jim Roper (after Glenn Dunnaway's disqualification) in the first race, followed by Byron, Bob Flock, Curtis Turner, Jack White, Byron again, Lee Petty, and Flock again.

From day one, France ruled NASCAR with an iron fist and his first rule was, "I make the rules." So, in spite of competing in four races in 1950 and five in 1951, Byron's name does not appear in the NASCAR record books for those two seasons because he raced in a couple of non-NASCAR events, and France stripped him of the points he had earned.

Whether he and France got along after that is a point lost in the mists of history, but it is likely that it didn't make any difference to Byron. In 1949, he proved to himself what he wanted to prove, and moved on to other things.

Byron volunteered for the Army Air Corps when World War II broke out, and served as a crewman on a B-24 Liberator bomber in the Aleutian Islands. He completed 57 missions successfully, but his luck ran out on the 58th. His plane was shot down over Kiska, and his

SEASON TO REMEMBER

Herb Thomas—1953

Herb Thomas was one of NASCAR's first great stars, winning championships in 1951 and '53 and finishing second in 1952, '54, and '56. He was also the first driver to win the Southern 500 three times (1951, '54, and '55). But his best year was 1953, when he won 12 times in 37 starts. He also won 12 poles and had an average starting position of 2.6. He had 27 top-five finishes and 31 top-10s on his way to a second championship in his "Fabulous Hudson Hornet."

left leg was so badly injured that the odds were against his ever walking again.

Byron spent 27 months in hospitals as doctors rebuilt his shattered leg. He told them that not only would he walk again, but he'd race, too.

When he did return to racing, it was with a specially designed boot that allowed his left foot to be strapped to the clutch. He walked with a noticeable limp (which, some said, became more pronounced in the presence of a beautiful woman), and had to be helped in and out of his car. That, more than anything else, led to his hanging up his driving helmet after the 1951 season.

He also had other things he wanted to try. Byron was interested in all types of racing, and he hooked up with millionaire Briggs Cunningham to develop a sports car capable of running against the best in the world. He later was manager of the Corvette racing team when GM had similar aspirations, but neither panned out. When he died in a Chicago hotel room in 1960 at the age of 45, Byron was manager of the Meisterbrauser Scarab SCCA team, about as far removed from his racing roots as he might have imagined.

So although most modern-day race fans could tell you the names of both of NASCAR's seven-time champions—Richard Petty and Dale Earnhardt—it might take more digging to find a fan who could tell you the first one.

And while there is a possibility that another seven-time champ is out there somewhere, there'll never be another first one.—J.M.

Absolutely Fabulous

They called them the "Fabulous Flocks." The trio of brothers from Fort Payne, Alabama, were part of NASCAR's infancy and among the reasons for the sport's early success.

Bob, Fonty (Fontello), and Tim Flock all put a mark on a fledgling sport in the wildest of its wild and wooly days. But for the entire Flock clan, "fabulous" fits. They were an adventurous breed whose name, if it was primarily linked to the racetrack, certainly was not limited to it.

Father Carl Lee was a trick cyclist and a tightrope walker. After his death in 1928, his oldest son, Carl Jr., left home to go to work for his uncle "Peachtree" Williams, who was noted as the largest bootlegger in Atlanta during Prohibition.

According to Tim Flock, Carl won the speedboat championship at the Chicago World's Fair in 1933. Carl's sister Reo was an airplane wing walker and stunt parachutist, and Ethel Flock Mobley, the youngest girl among the nine Flock children, raced against her brothers on occasion.

Two of the three racing brothers' driving careers began on the back roads of north Georgia. The family followed Bob to Atlanta, where he was making daily runs of illegal whiskey from the hills into Atlanta. Fonty delivered corn liquor on his bicycle until he was old enough to drive, and then he too took to the roads.

Tim, the youngest of the three, never drove a whiskey car. But he occasionally tagged along with his brothers when they joined others in the whiskey trade around Atlanta for impromptu races at makeshift tracks to see whose car was the fastest.

Bob Flock was a fearless driver with steely blue eyes who won hundreds of races in modified cars mostly in the era before NASCAR was formed. He also was an indefatigable competitor. In the final race of the 1951 NASCAR season on November 25 in Mobile, Alabama, Bob's car flipped. He was injured, but he didn't know how badly, so he drove home to Pensacola, Florida. He was in such pain that he went to the doctor and was told he had fractured several ribs. A week later, the pain had not abated, so he went to another doctor, who discovered that he had driven the 55 miles from Mobile to Pensacola with a broken neck!

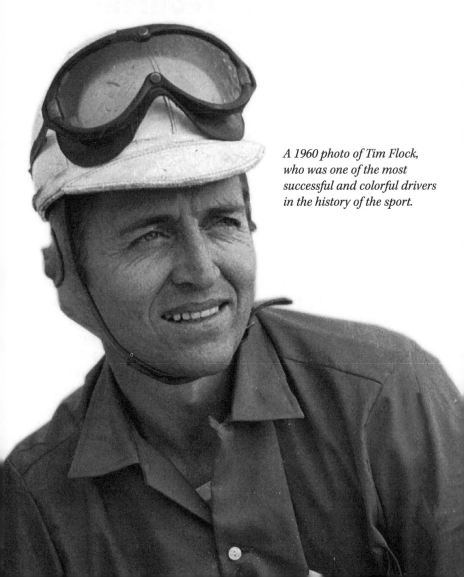

A 1960 photo of Tim Flock, who was one of the most successful and colorful drivers in the history of the sport.

It was nearly a year before he got behind the wheel of another race car, but at Asheville-Weaverville (North Carolina) Speedway on August 17, 1952, Bob won the race, finishing two laps ahead of his closest competitor, his brother Tim.

TRIVIA

The last victory of Tim Flock's driving career came on the Road America road course at Elkhart Lake, Wisconsin, on August 12, 1956. One other factor made it more special. What was that?

Answers to the trivia questions are on pages 180–181.

Where Bob was withdrawn, Fonty was gregarious and a crowd-pleaser. During hot weather, he occasionally raced wearing Bermuda shorts and loud shirts. When he won the Southern 500 in 1952, he stopped his big Oldsmobile on the front straightaway, climbed up on the hood, and led the crowd in a stirring rendition of "Dixie."

Of the three, it was Tim who was destined for stardom. He became NASCAR's third champion in 1952, and in 1955 set a standard that was not matched until Richard Petty came along a generation later. Driving one of Carl Kiekhaefer's immaculate Chrysler 300s, Tim became a sensation. He won 18 poles and 18 races in the 38 races (of 45) in which he competed and beat Buck Baker for the 1955 championship by 1,508 points.

Kiekhaefer owned Mercury Outboard Motors and had the idea that stock-car racing would be a good way to advertise his product and maybe provide a little knowledge about engines that could be adapted to his boat motors. Kiekhaefer approached racing with the kind of professionalism that wouldn't become common in NASCAR for years. He hired meteorologists to travel with his team. He took soil samples at each dirt track and had them analyzed to be better prepared when his cars raced on similar tracks. And, unheard of even today, he allowed his drivers to keep all their winnings.

Kiekhaefer came not only to win but also to dominate. He entered cars in 40 races in 1955 and won 22 of them. In a 300-mile race at Memphis-Arkansas Speedway that year, Kiekhaefer entered four of his own cars (driven by the Flock brothers and Norm Nelson) and sponsored nearly every other frontrunner as well, including winner Speedy Thompson.

SEASON TO REMEMBER

Tim Flock—1955

When Carl Kiekhaefer came into NASCAR for the 1955 season, he hired the popular and successful Tim Flock to drive his No. 300 Chrysler. In their first race together, Flock led every one of the 34 laps to win on the beach-and-road course in Daytona and was off to one of the greatest seasons in history. He won 18 times in 39 starts, and in a remarkable 11 of those victories he led every lap. Flock led 3,495 of the 6,208 laps he ran that year and also won 18 poles on his way to a championship.

If Kiekhaefer took the racing world by storm by winning 22 races in 1955, he brought it to its knees in 1956 when his teams won 30 of 48 races. Kiekhaefer added hard-nosed Buck Baker to a stable that included Thompson and Tim Flock and eventually Herb Thomas, the 1951 and 1953 champion.

Kiekhaefer's problem was that he was a perfectionist and ran his operation like a military organization. He often rented entire hotels for his teams, putting the drivers and mechanics on one side and their wives and girlfriends on the other, and did not allow fraternization among the ranks. He had bed checks. The drivers of that day (or any day, for that matter) chafed under Kiekhaefer's autocratic hand. By April, Tim Flock had had enough. Even after winning three of the first 10 races, Flock quit.

"My ulcers were tearing me up," Flock said. "I was always on standby. Never had any time to myself."

Thomas was hired to replace Flock and won four races, but he too left the team. And that decision helped lead to the end of the Kiekhaefer empire.

Baker was the team's most successful driver in 1956, winning 14 races and the championship. But after leaving the Kiekhaefer team, Thomas was still contending for the driver's title.

Kiekhaefer was determined that Thomas wasn't going to beat Baker. He rented a track in Shelby, North Carolina, and convinced

NASCAR to add a race on a previously scheduled open date in October. During that race, Thomas was involved in a bad crash with Speedy Thompson, Baker's Kiekhaefer teammate, and was critically injured.

Baker went on to win the title, but because of the backlash from the incident at Shelby and from the way his teams were dominating the sport, Kiekhaefer packed up and left NASCAR after just two seasons.

Kiekhaefer got into racing for one reason: to sell outboards. The thing he had not counted on was the American public's distaste for a bully. By the end of the 1956 season, his drivers were booed more often than they heard cheers, and his outboard sales never rose appreciably. So with the same suddenness with which he had come into racing, Kiekhaefer disappeared.

The Flocks were fading out, too. Fonty quit driving for good after a serious crash at Darlington in 1957, and Tim raced only sporadically after the 1956 season.

TRIVIA

What historic event happened in the Turkey Day 200 on December 1, 1963, in Jacksonville, Florida?

Answers to the trivia questions are on pages 180–181.

In 1961, driver-entrepreneur Curtis Turner attempted to organize a drivers' union under the Teamsters, and Tim Flock backed him all the way. France banned both for life. Turner eventually was allowed back into NASCAR's good graces, but Flock never was.—J.M.

Racing's Royal Family

There's a shade of blue somewhere between the color of the sky and that of a robin's egg. It's called "Petty blue" and anybody who knows anything about NASCAR's history could pick it out from the distance of half a straightaway. Lee Petty and then his son, Richard, made the hue famous by driving race cars painted that color to victory after victory after victory in stock car racing's first series.

How did the first family of racing come across the perfect shade? Well, in the early days of his racing career, Lee wanted to paint his car blue, but he didn't have enough paint to do the job. He did, however, have some white paint, so he mixed the white with the blue and a trademark was born.

The roots of the Petty racing legacy, unmatched though it might be, are pretty much just that simple, too. It all started in 1948. Lee Petty and his brother, Julian, put a Chrysler engine in a 1937 Plymouth and went racing. Lee won. And the Pettys just got used to it.

"We're racers," Richard said in 1999, as the family marked its 50th year of NASCAR competition. "That's all we ever knew and all we ever wanted to be.... Farmers don't go out and start building houses. They've always got something growing in the backyard. We're the same."

The Pettys' racing backyard is near the tiny North Carolina town of Randleman—actually closer to a wide place in the road called Level Cross.

Petty Enterprises is still located there, beside the house where Lee lived and Richard grew up. The team's first "race shop" was a shed where farm equipment was sheltered. If you know where to look, you can still see the A-frame roof of that shed at the team's complex.

SEASON TO REMEMBER

Lee Petty—1959

The crowning season of Lee Petty's brilliant career included his dramatic victory over Johnny Beauchamp in the inaugural Daytona 500. It was the first of 11 victories in 42 races for Petty in a year where he averaged a finish of 6.2 with 27 top-fives and 35 top-10s. The places where Petty won that year read like a history book of NASCAR's great venues of the era—he won twice at North Wilkesboro, twice at Columbia (South Carolina) Speedway, and once each at Martinsville Speedway, legendary Lakewood Speedway in Atlanta, the Southern States Fairgrounds in Charlotte, Bowman Gray Stadium in Winston-Salem, and Hickory Motor Speedway.

When NASCAR started its Strictly Stock series with a race in Charlotte in June of 1949, Petty borrowed a Buick from a friend, piled up the family and a few tools, and headed down the road. Other members of the family came down in Lee's car. In the race, Lee wrecked and tore up the Buick, leaving just one car for the return trip. There wasn't enough room for everybody to get home in Lee's car, so Richard, just shy of his 12th birthday, had to hitchhike his way back.

Lee Petty won the seventh race in the history of what's now the Nextel Cup Series, at Heidelberg Raceway in Pennsylvania. He won at least one race in each of the first 13 seasons in the circuit's history, earning championships in 1954, 1958, and 1959.

Lee also won the very first Daytona 500 in 1959, in a dramatic battle with Johnny Beauchamp on the final lap. Lee won 11 races and his third championship that year, and then won five more times in the 1960 season when he finished sixth in the standings—his worst finish in NASCAR's first 12 years. Late that year, in what was counted as the second race of the 1961 season, Petty won at Jacksonville, Florida, for his 54th career victory.

The next February, he and Beauchamp were racing each other again at Daytona in a qualifying race before the 500. Their cars

SEASON TO REMEMBER

Richard Petty—1971

There will never be another five-year period in NASCAR like the one Richard Petty capped off with his third career championship in 1971. After winning 27 races in 1967, Petty followed that with 16, 10, and 18 more wins in the next three years. Then he won the Daytona 500—for the third time—and 20 more races in 1971. He also finished in the top five 38 times in 46 races.

locked together, crashed through the guardrail, and wound up in the parking lot. Petty was injured badly and spent four months in the hospital. Although he drove a few times after that, the time had come to pass the torch.

Richard had run his first race in NASCAR's top series in 1958 in Toronto, crashing and finishing 17th in a race his father won. He won for the first time at the Southern States Fairgrounds track in Charlotte in February 1960, and he won two more races that year.

Richard, who along with his brother, Maurice, had worked on Lee's cars while growing up, quickly made it clear the Pettys were not through dominating the sport. Richard won at least one race in each of his 18 seasons starting in 1960. That means that Lee or Richard Petty won races in every single year from 1949, when the Cup series began, through 1977.

Before he retired after the final race of 1992, Petty, nicknamed "the King," had won 200 races—95 more than anyone else in history—and seven championships. He won a record 27 races in 1967, including 10 in a row, another record. He won 21 times in 1971 and then set a record for victories in the "modern era" with 13 in 1975.

Richard won the Daytona 500 seven times. He won 15 races at Martinsville, 15 at North Wilkesboro, 13 at Richmond, and 11 at Rockingham. He won at least one race at 51 different tracks.

By 1984, after surviving wicked crashes and a couple of manufacturer's boycotts that once saw him spend part of a season in drag racing, Petty had won 199 races. That July Fourth at Daytona,

President Ronald Reagan was coming to the track to see the race and gave the command for the cars to fire engines from Air Force One. He got there in time to see Petty race Cale Yarborough back to a caution flag with three laps to go, edging Yarborough by a fender to win for the 200th time.

Despite all of those accomplishments, however, Petty's greatest contribution to the sport might be the approach he brought to dealing with his fans. It has been said that with the possible exception of boxing champion Muhammad Ali, nobody has ever signed more autographs than the King. Still, it was the racing that kept Petty going for a record 1,185 starts before he stepped away at the end of the 1992 season.

Richard Petty (right) walks down the pit road with his son, Kyle, during the early 1980s.

"To tell the truth, I just love climbing in a race car and driving it," Petty said. "All the rest of what I do, signing autographs, giving interviews, making public appearances, visiting fan clubs, that's all something I could do without, but it's all part of the business.

"Racing is the time I enjoy myself the most. When I'm strapped in that car, riding up along the high bank, there's nobody in the world who is going to bother me, except, of course, maybe another driver. But it's my time, my private time, and I still enjoy doing it.

"I heard people saying maybe I ought to retire, that maybe I hung on too long, but they didn't understand what racing means to me."

The end of Richard's driving career, however, did not mean the end of the Petty empire.

Kyle, Richard's son, made his first career start in 1979 at Talladega. He got his first victory driving for the Wood Brothers at Richmond in 1986 and won eight times in his career, all while driving for teams other than Petty Enterprises. In 47 seasons, from 1949 through 1995, Lee, Richard, or Kyle Petty won at least one race in 41 of those seasons.

At the start of the 1997 season, Kyle returned to the family business, and over the past decade he has taken the lead role in shaping the family's team for its future. The plan was for Kyle's son, Adam, to become the fourth-generation Petty to drive the family's cars. Adam had raced in the American Speed Association and Automobile Racing Club of America series and in April 2000 at the age of 19 he ran his first Nextel Cup race at Texas Motor Speedway.

"When Adam was 16, he begged me to let him drive around Darlington during a test," Kyle said. "We were in a street car and I

DID YOU KNOW . . . On June 14, 1959, Richard Petty took the checkered flag at Lakewood Speedway near Atlanta and believed that he'd won his first victory in NASCAR's top series? But another driver challenged the scoring, claiming he'd actually completed the race first. NASCAR officials investigated and reversed their call, awarding the victory to the driver making the protest—Lee Petty, Richard's father. "I didn't really question it since it was family," Richard said. "I guess I'd still be there arguing about it if it were someone else."

IF ONLY . . . They had not missed each other by maybe 10 minutes, Kyle and Adam Petty may have been on the same racetrack at the same time. From the time Adam Petty decided he wanted to go into the "family business" and drive race cars, he looked forward to the day that he and his father, Kyle, would be on the track together in NASCAR's top series.

On April 2, 2000, 19-year-old Adam started his first Nextel Cup race at Texas Motor Speedway. He lined up 33rd in the starting lineup for the DirecTV 500. But his father wasn't in the starting lineup. Kyle, in the No. 44 Pontiac, hadn't gone fast enough in qualifying to make the 43-car field.

Kyle stayed in Texas to watch his son race, of course, and when Elliott Sadler needed a relief driver Kyle was asked to step into the No. 21 Ford owned by the Wood Brothers.

But on Lap 216, Adam's engine failed and he pulled his car into the garage. A few minutes later, as the leaders were completing their 228th lap, Kyle drove out of the garage in relief of Sadler.

"I thought my dream might come true for a minute," Adam said that day.

Adam was scheduled to try to make his second start a little more than a month later at Lowe's Motor Speedway. But he was killed in a crash during a Busch Series practice session at New Hampshire International Speedway before he got the chance.

Richard Petty wasn't at Texas to see what turned out to be his grandson's only career Cup start. He was back home in North Carolina with his father, Lee, who was ill. Lee Petty died three days later.

was sitting there telling him what to do. He ran the car as hard as he could, got as close to the wall as he could, and the look on his face was amazing. I thought, 'Do I get that much pleasure out of this stuff?' I knew right then what he was going to do."

Later that spring, however, as he practiced for a NASCAR Busch Series race at New Hampshire International Speedway, Adam's throttle hung open as he drove down the back stretch and he slammed into the Turn 3 wall. Adam was killed.

The tragedy shook not only the Petty family but also the entire racing world. Kyle Petty moved to the No. 45 cars that he was preparing for his son, and over the past few years he has been working

SEASON TO REMEMBER

Richard Petty—1975

"The King" already had the record for victories in a single season, so it seemed only right that he also set the record for the most wins (13) in one year for the modern era, after the schedule was trimmed. Petty won four of the season's first seven races and later added victories in the World 600 at Charlotte and in the Firecracker 400 at Daytona in July. For good measure, he also racked up his sixth career championship and his fourth in five seasons.

diligently to bring the competitive level of the cars fielded by Petty Enterprises back toward the sport's top tier, hiring former Nextel Cup champion Bobby Labonte to drive the famed No. 43 cars for the 2006 season and beyond.

"I'm not sure time heals things as much as time gives you ways to deal with it," Kyle said. "But it doesn't soften it. It doesn't take the sharp edges off."

Like his grandfather and father, Kyle's contributions to the sport and to the world don't stop at the outside walls of the racetrack. Before his death, Adam had visited a camp for critically ill children in Florida and told his parents he thought it would be a great idea if they opened a similar facility near their home in North Carolina. Kyle and his wife, Pattie, went to work after Adam was killed to make that dream a reality. Now the Victory Junction Gang camp stands as a living memorial to the young man remembered for his smile and his joy for life.

"The Petty family is a national racing treasure," two-time Winston Cup champion Darrell Waltrip said. "If our newer fans want to understand and appreciate the essence of this sport, they need to look back at our history and see their contributions."—D.P.

A Pair but Not Two of a Kind

With nicknames like the "Blond Blizzard" and the "Clown Prince of Racing," Curtis Turner and Joe Weatherly were as incongruous a pair of racers as you might find. But in the early days of NASCAR racing, neither was hard to find.

Turner was 6'2" with wavy hair, an on-again, off-again millionaire who raced just for the hell of it and could charm the rattles off a diamondback.

"Little Joe" Weatherly, maybe 5'7" in the saddle oxfords he wore when he raced, was a pugnacious-looking former motorcycle champion who once won a NASCAR championship by bumming rides.

As improbable a match as you might imagine, the two Virginians—Turner was from Floyd and Weatherly from Norfolk—nonetheless captured a generation of race fans with their derring-do off the racetrack as much as on it.

The only thing they loved more than beating and banging on the track was chasing women when the race was over. Their exploits are the stuff of legend, but there are a few hard facts. Turner never won a Grand National championship, but from NASCAR's first season until his last win in 1965 he won 18 races, 16 poles, and a legion of fans who consider him nothing less than the greatest driver to ever compete in a stock car.

With the number of races NASCAR ran in those days, Turner's victory total might not seem all that impressive until you consider that Turner never raced a whole season and was banned from the sport for four years. Plus, Turner didn't race for championships. He raced to win races.

In 1956, for instance, NASCAR's most ambitious season included 48 Grand National races and 45 races on the short-lived convertible circuit. Turner drove in 42 convertible races, and won 22 of them. He drove in only 13 Grand National events, but his sole victory in that league was the big one—the Southern 500 at Darlington, which at the time was the sport's most prestigious event.

In those days, as now, NASCAR's points system valued consistency and attendance more than wins, so Turner did not win the convertible championship. He missed three races and lost out to Bob Welborn for the title.

Not winning a championship didn't bother Turner so much. His greatest disappointment came off the track. The high-living Turner

Curtis Turner rounds the south turn in his Ford as he makes the transition from paved road onto the beach during his winning lap of the Convertible Stock Car Race at Daytona Beach on February 25, 1956.

Joe Weatherly stands by the 1939 Ford that he drove to fourth place in the 100-mile stock car race at Daytona Beach in February 1952.

made several fortunes in the timber business—and spent them—but the only time he was ever truly beaten was when he decided to build a racetrack.

Long story short, Turner scraped together loans in 1960 to begin construction on what today is Lowe's Motor Speedway in Charlotte, North Carolina, but he stretched himself too thin. When it appeared that he would still come up short, he tried to borrow $800,000 from the Teamsters Union in return for his attempt to unionize the drivers. There he ran head-on into Bill France Sr., NASCAR's founder and president. France hated unions with a passion. He vowed that he would never submit to a union, and banned Turner for life.

Ironically, up to that point, the two men had been close friends, and even copiloted a Nash in the inaugural Mexican Road Race in 1950. Their parting was bitter, and even though France reinstated Turner in 1965, it was more a measure of Turner's enormous popularity with race fans than one of reconciliation between the two. France needed Turner, and Turner needed to race.

TOP 10

Victory Leaders in NASCAR's Premier Series (1960–69)

	Driver	Wins	Races	Top 5s	Poles	Earnings
1.	Richard Petty	101	449	263	82	$789,363
2.	David Pearson	57	332	176	52	$669,093
3.	Ned Jarrett	48	325	181	35	$344,581
4.	Junior Johnson	34	203	81	41	$262,520
5.	Fred Lorenzen	26	122	64	30	$419,122
6.	Joe Weatherly	24	159	82	16	$217,858
7.	Bobby Isaac	21	171	70	23	$220,592
8.	Rex White	21	155	79	22	$189,716
9.	Jim Paschal	18	200	87	5	$240,825
10.	Bobby Allison	16	154	62	9	$208,870

Source: www.racing-reference.info

Weatherly, on the other hand, won 25 Grand National races between his first at Nashville, Tennessee, in 1958 and his last at Hillsborough, North Carolina, in 1963, as well as 12 convertible races from 1956 to 1959. He won two of those Grand National championships (1962 and 1963) as much with guts as with talent

Weatherly hooked up with car owner Bud Moore for the 1962 season and, in first-class equipment, he won nine races. Even more remarkable, he finished out of the top 10 only seven times in the 52-race season.

What he did in 1963 was more remarkable. Moore decided to run only the big races that season, and Weatherly hitched rides with any car owner who didn't have a driver when Moore wasn't there. In spite of missing one race and running 19 more in inferior equipment, Weatherly's dogged determination won him a title.

When he couldn't find a seat for the May race at Richmond, Virginia's Southside Speedway, Weatherly dropped to 2,274 points behind Richard Petty—barely six weeks after he'd won in Moore's car at Richmond Fairgrounds.

However, picking up rides with eight other team owners (including one whose name never has found its way into NASCAR's record books), Weatherly fought his way back to the top. He didn't clinch the championship until the final race of the season. His seventh-place finish in the Golden State 400 at Riverside Raceway in California on November 16, 1963, was enough to hold off Petty for the title.

TRIVIA

The Cup circuit held its first night race in 1951 in Columbia, South Carolina, on a short track. When and where was the first night race at a superspeedway, a track one mile or longer, held?

Answers to the trivia questions are on pages 180–181.

Sometime during that trying season, Weatherly made a statement that summed up what a racer should be.

"Listen," Weatherly said. "I'd rather play the rabbit than the dog any day. But if I can't be the rabbit, it doesn't mean I'm going to give up the chase."

Turner and Weatherly were dog-eat-dog competitors on the track, but inseparable off the track. Turner loved women and Canadian Club whiskey almost as much as he loved driving a race car. At their "party pad" in Daytona Beach, a ramshackle apartment the two shared during NASCAR's Speedweeks, Weatherly dispensed the CC with a fire extinguisher, and the two kept score on a chalkboard of the women they bedded.

The two tore up so many rental cars racing against each other on the streets—"Little Joe" also had a penchant for running them into motel pools—that rental agencies posted their photos in offices all over the country with the stern admonition never to rent a car to either one.

It is never "fitting" that a race car driver die violently, but it is hard to imagine either of the two men growing old gracefully, sitting in rocking chairs and telling tall tales to their grandkids.

TRIVIA

Races in what is now the NASCAR Nextel Cup Series have been held in 36 different states. Which 12 of the continental United States have not hosted a race?

Answers to the trivia questions are on pages 180–181.

Neither did.

Weatherly, only two and a half months after he had won the 1963 championship, died in a crash on the same track, Riverside, at which he'd locked up his last title.

Turner, ever the wheeler-dealer, died in 1970 after flying one of his business cronies, Bob Baughman, home to Pennsylvania. He and golf pro/friend Clarence King, returning to Charlotte after dropping off Baughman, crashed into a hillside near Punxsutawney, Pennsylvania.—J.M.

Win until You're Done

As long as Junior Johnson is around, NASCAR history lives.

Like the sport that made him famous, the man from Ingle Hollow, North Carolina, has come a long, long way in life. At age 75, he's a country gentleman who has left racing and all he accomplished there in his rearview mirror.

Not long after a divorce from his first wife, Flossie, in 1992, Johnson sold the race teams with which he'd won 139 races and six championships.

He married again, and he and his considerably younger wife have since had two young children. Johnson is perfectly content these days to hang around Wilkes County, which he once called the "best place in the world, I don't care where you go," and watch them grow up.

It's not that Johnson turned his back on racing. He still shows up here and there, sometimes when somebody wants to give him an award aimed at reminding people just how great Johnson was, and sometimes when he just wants to drop in and see how the circus is running these days.

Fans who've discovered NASCAR in the past decade or so might not completely understand just how well Johnson personifies the sport's development from its early backwoods beginnings to the modern-day extravaganza that it has become.

Johnson's story begins right around the place he calls home right now, the hills of western North Carolina. Born in 1931, he was the middle child of seven for Robert and Lora Belle Johnson. Robert Glen Johnson Jr. helped his daddy around the farm and also quickly learned how to drive a car to help deliver the product of the family

TOP 10

All-Time Leaders in Winning Percentage among Drivers with 100 or More Career Starts*

	Driver	Wins	Races	Pct.
1.	Herb Thomas	48	228	.211
2.	Tim Flock	39	187	.209
3.	David Pearson	105	574	.183
4.	Richard Petty	200	1,184	.169
5.	Jeff Gordon	73	437	.167
6.	Fred Lorenzen	26	158	.165
7.	Fireball Roberts	33	206	.160
	Junior Johnson	50	313	.160†
9.	Cale Yarborough	83	560	.148
10.	Ned Jarrett	50	352	.142

* Through the 2005 season.

business—that untaxed and otherwise unauthorized alcoholic elixir known as moonshine.

By age 14, Johnson was flying across back roads and down secret dirt shortcuts and escape routes through the woods of the hills around home. It wasn't racing, but it wasn't recreation. If Johnson got caught, jail wasn't the only consequence to worry about. There was also the loss of perfectly good 'shine, which would be confiscated or destroyed. That took money out of the Johnson family's coffers, and there was little to spare.

Johnson was 17 the day his brother L.B. Johnson came to the field where Junior was plowing, barefoot, behind a mule. Cars were racing down the road at the North Wilkesboro track, L.B. said. Nobody could drive better than Junior, L.B. figured, so he told his brother to go see if he couldn't make a little money, legally.

Johnson drove in his first race in NASCAR's top series at Darlington in 1953, crashing out after 110 laps and finishing 38th in a 59-car field. He ran four times in 1954 and then 36 times in 45 races in 1955. Johnson got his first career win at Hickory Motor Speedway and added four more victories that year.

But in 1956, Johnson's budding NASCAR career took an unfortunate turn. It was an open secret in Wilkes County that the Johnsons were in the moonshine business, and agents searched the family's house often enough that Johnson's mother would serve some of them coffee and pie on their visits. Robert Johnson Sr. spent nearly a third of his life in jail for various infractions, and in 1956 agents found the family's still. They also found Junior there, and that resulted in a two-year prison sentence. Johnson was shipped off to Ohio, where he served 11 months.

Junior Johnson peers from his car after winning the pole position for the Dixie 400 stock car race at the Atlanta International Raceway in 1964. Johnson qualified for the $56,000 race with a four-lap speed of 145.906 mph.

Johnson got out in time to run one NASCAR race in October 1957 at North Wilkesboro. The next season, he won twice at his home track and at one point won four times in five starts.

Before stepping away from driving with 50 career victories in 1966, Johnson's biggest win came in the 1960 Daytona 500. It was there that he "discovered" the phenomenon of drafting.

Johnson's car owner from 1959 had pulled out of the sport, but barely a week before the Daytona 500 Johnson got a call from Raymond Fox, a legendary car builder based in Daytona. A business-man had come to Fox and asked him to build a car and get a driver to run in the 500. Johnson agreed to come see what he could do.

Fox built Johnson a Chevrolet, and it was painfully slow—nearly 30 mph slower than the speediest Pontiacs. Johnson was about to go home, but Fox promised to find some more speed, and Johnson took the Chevy back on the track. He got in behind Cotton Owens, who was in one of the much faster Pontiacs, and stayed with him. Johnson didn't think Fox could have improved the car that much, so he tried a run by himself and found he was as slow as he'd ever been.

The more Johnson rode around behind Pontiacs, the more he figured out that it was an aerodynamic effect from running behind the faster car that was pulling him along. He told nobody, not even Fox, what he'd found, and on race day he shadowed every fast Pontiac he could get a bumper to. Finally, he followed Bobby Johns long enough to get the lead and gain track position. But Johns, getting a tow from a fellow Pontiac driver's lapped car as others figured out what Johnson was up to, passed Johnson on Lap 170.

Johnson was still holding on to Johns's rear bumper. "Then, coming off the second turn with 10 laps to go, one of the damndest things happened I ever saw on a track," Johnson said in his biogra-phy, *Brave in Life*, written by Tom Higgins and Steve Waid. "The back glass popped out of Bobby's car and flew into the air. I think our speed and the traffic combined to create a vacuum that sucked that back glass right out. The sudden change in the airflow around Bobby's car caused him to spin into the grass along the backstretch. By the time he got straightened out...I was long gone."

Because Johnson never ran a full schedule, he never won a cham-pionship as a driver. But he took care of that after beginning his

TOP 10

Winningest Owners in NASCAR Nextel Cup History*

Owner/Team	Wins	Races	All-Time Earnings
1. Petty Enterprises	268	2,726	$68,166,721
2. Rick Hendrick	147	2,204	$202,058,742
3. Junior Johnson	132	1,049	$23,646,744
4. Wood Brothers	97	1,264	$38,253,580
5. Holman-Moody	96	528	$2,086,623
6. Jack Roush	94	2,023	$214,959,897
7. Richard Childress	81	1,515	$129,009,246
8. Bud Moore	63	960	$15,749,067
9. Robert Yates	57	953	$99,487,908
10. Roger Penske	55	835	$82,564,836

* As of September 22, 2006.

Source: www.racing-reference.info

career as a car owner in 1965, owning the No. 26 Fords that he drove to 12 victories.

Johnson was out of the sport briefly in the early 1970s, but in the middle of the 1984 season he bought a team owned by Richard Howard that featured Cale Yarborough as its driver. Yarborough won three times that year, then won 28 races and an unprecedented three straight titles from 1976 to 1978.

Three years later, Darrell Waltrip moved into the seat of what was by then the No. 11 Buicks and won championships in 1981, 1982, and 1985. In six years together, before Waltrip left to join Hendrick Motorsports for the 1987 season, he and Johnson won 43 races together.

Neil Bonnett, Geoff Bodine, and Terry Labonte all won races driving for Johnson before he flirted with another championship in 1992 when Bill Elliott won five races and led the championship race until faltering late in the season.

Jimmy Spencer's victory in the No. 27 Ford at Talladega in July 1994 was the final victory for Johnson as a NASCAR car owner. Brett

DID YOU KNOW . . . NASCAR founder Bill France Sr. saw Junior Johnson's potential as a driver and urged him to commit to racing full-time? But Johnson had other ideas.

"I told Mr. France that I was involved in racing, but I wasn't committed to it," Johnson said.

France asked Johnson to describe the difference.

"I said, 'Well, it's like if you have bacon and eggs for breakfast,'" Johnson said. "'That chicken is involved. But that pig? He's committed.'"

Bodine drove the famed No. 11 car for Johnson in 1995, with several drivers splitting time in the other car. After that year, Johnson sold his team to Bodine.

In 1998, as NASCAR marked its 50th anniversary season, Johnson was named one of the sport's 50 greatest drivers. *Sports Illustrated* went one better, putting him in the number one slot on its list of best drivers in history. He's in every kind of stock car racing hall of fame that's ever been established, and he'll no doubt be part of the new official NASCAR Hall of Fame that is scheduled to open in Charlotte, North Carolina, in 2010.

That'll be just fine with Johnson, but he'd also be just fine if racing forgot about him—as though that were possible.

"My career was great but it was time to move on," he said. "If I'm done with something, I'm done with it."—D.P.

Wizards with Wrenches

Race car drivers get a lot of credit for driving cars at 200 mph, and they should. It takes guts to go that fast.

But race car drivers would be nowhere without race car mechanics; those wizards who, by means both legal and shady, squeeze every last ounce out of an engine and fudge on the chassis and car bodies to shave hundredths of a second off lap times.

Those men who added to the safety of race cars should get full marks, certainly, but safety is dull stuff. Nothing captures the imagination of race fans quite so much as those masters of the "gray areas" of the rule book.

Dale Inman, the crew chief on Richard Petty's cars, once "engineered" a win by simply switching the left- and right-side tires on Petty's car.

Gary Nelson was so clever a mechanic that NASCAR figured it was better to have him working to catch violations than dreaming up tricks they couldn't catch, so they hired him as the Winston Cup Series director.

And Maurice "Pop" Eargle, who worked for car owner Bud Moore, once solved the problem of a race car sitting too low by surreptitiously dropping a small rock in front of the wheel, rolling the front tire onto it, and asking the inspector to please measure again.

But there were no two better practitioners of the black art than Henry "Smokey" Yunick and Robert "Junior" Johnson.

Johnson was named the best driver of NASCAR's first 50 years by *Sports Illustrated*, but his 50-win driving career paled in comparison to his record as a hands-on team owner. Most of his driving career was spent in cars not owned by him, but he hit his stride as an owner.

Johnson's cars won 132 races, which, at the time he retired in 1998, was still second on the all-time win list. Two of his drivers, Cale Yarborough and Darrell Waltrip, each won three championships under Johnson's banner.

Johnson knew more about race cars than just about anybody and if he'd never admit to breaking rules outright, he didn't mind bending them to his advantage. If it wasn't covered by a rule, it was fair game. And the thing he liked least was NASCAR's changing the rules in the middle of the contest.

"If you go out here and figure out how to do something better than somebody else, you deserve to get the benefit of it, not to be stomped in the ground because you've got it," Johnson once said. "Cheating is not always what it really is; it's innovation and safety and that kind of stuff."

Johnson's quiet demeanor and slow drawl gave some the impression that he was little more than a country hick, but that was misleading. He had a brilliant mechanical mind, and what he termed "rootin' around under the hood" was some pretty heady stuff.

One investigative reporter who came to his Wilkes County, North Carolina, shops couldn't believe the degree of sophistication of Johnson's operation. He somewhat smugly opined that Johnson must have spent a lot of time with the engineers in Detroit.

"Naw," Johnson said. "They come to me."

If Detroit came to Johnson, the world came to Yunick. When your hometown is Daytona Beach—the self-proclaimed "World Center of Speed"—and the sign in front of your shop says, "Best Damn Garage in Town," the world will find you.

In the late 1960s, the automakers in Detroit wanted Yunick's innovative mind so much that Ford offered him a $500,000-a-year contract for five years, and GM trumped the offer with $585,000 a year—for life. But Yunick was something of a cowboy in that he longed for the wide-open spaces, and he walked out on both deals.

With only a 10th-grade education, Yunick may have been the sole pure genius in racing's early years, even if that genius at times only concerned itself with getting around NASCAR's rules.

The only thing Yunick liked more than tweaking the rules was tweaking the nose of Bill France Sr., NASCAR's founder. The two

The Wood Brothers racing team made a name for itself inside NASCAR racing, but in 1965 they revolutionized Indy Car racing at the same time?

Lotus team owner Colin Chapman wanted an edge for his Ford-powered entry driven by Scot Jimmy Clark in the Indianapolis 500, and the Woods gave him one no one would forget.

The Woods were noted for quick pit stops, so they went to Indianapolis to pit Clark's car. Pit stop speed was not at a premium, but when the Woods had a week to work on it, they made Indy racing a whole new game.

Clark pitted for fuel (alcohol, in 1965) twice, and he spent a total of 43 seconds in the pits. Unheard of. In 1965, one set of treaded tires lasted 500 miles, so fuel was the only concern.

Team owner Leonard Wood recalled that the team spent the week practicing the best way to hook and unhook the three-inch fuel hoses that gravity-fed the alcohol into the car. The nozzle had to be pushed in and then locked in order to function, and he said they filed and polished the connectors. Today they'd call it "ergonomics," but back then it was just plain common sense.

Two men held up the fuel line to maximize flow, and polished connectors worked better than unpolished ones. Because Clark spent less time in the pits, he beat Parnelli Jones to the checkers by nearly two minutes.

Indy was a different world. This was back in the days of hearty handshakes and socks on the shoulder. When they got to victory lane, Leonard Wood said, "I remember Chapman—he just hugged everybody and that was sort of unusual. It was great to go."

men never liked each other, but they held a grudging respect for the other's abilities.

The venue changes according to the teller, but there is a nugget of truth in the tale about the time NASCAR officials almost tore one of Yunick's cars apart seeking infractions. The inspection included completely removing the gas tank. When their fine-toothed inspection was over the officials informed him they had found a dozen violations. Whereupon Yunick climbed through the window of the car, fired up the engine, growled, "Make that 13!" and drove away—with the gas tank sitting on the inspection table!

Where Johnson and Yunick differed was that Johnson was primarily concerned with race cars. Yunick had an interest in anything mechanical and had nearly a dozen U.S. patents to show for it.

He did extensive work with a "hot vapor" engine that could have revolutionized the automobile industry with fuel savings and cleaner emissions. In his three-volume autobiography, Yunick wrote that he pursued that because "I notice I got kids and relatives who

Smokey Yunick (right), considered a genius mechanic during NASCAR's early years, poses with driver Herb Thomas and their trophy from Darlington in 1954.

TOP 10

All-Time Leaders in Pole Positions Earned*

1.	Richard Petty	123
2.	David Pearson	112
3.	Cale Yarborough	69
4.	Darrell Waltrip	59
5.	Bobby Allison	58
6.	Bill Elliott	55
7.	Jeff Gordon	54
8.	Bobby Isaac	49
9.	Junior Johnson	46
10.	Buck Baker	45

* Through the 2005 season.

Source: NASCAR Statistical Services

may end up living in a cold dark world. I decide to help devise a plan to double the usefulness of a barrel of crude oil or its equivalent in gas. Enter 25 years of the Smokey BTU juggling contest."

Yunick built working models and installed them in cars, but for reasons never explained (he tweaked a few noses in Detroit along they way, too), the engine never reached mass production. Toward the end of his life, Yunick could be seen at NASCAR tracks, wearing his simple white mechanic's outfit and trademark flat-topped Stetson, scribbling on yellow legal pads. As it turned out, it was his autobiography.

At the conclusion of the chapter about what could have been his lasting gift to his fellow man, Yunick the iconoclast came through loud and clear.

"As it stands today," he wrote, "the Smithsonian has inquired about a hot vapor engine for their museum. Maybe you can go check it out there if they ever get into vehicles. They've also got one of my hats."—J.M.

Dreamers and Doers

If it had been left up to the nine-to-five crowd, NASCAR would still be riding around the little dirt "bullrings" that dotted county fairgrounds around the South in the 1940s and would no doubt draw about as much attention today as they did back then.

But NASCAR had visionaries who were also doers. And if Harold Brasington was a dreamer, then Bill France dreamed in Technicolor. Between those two, the two most significant racetracks in NASCAR history—heck, two of the most significant tracks in the history of racing—became places where no stock car racer worth his salt hasn't dreamed of winning.

Brasington, an earth mover by trade, made a proposal during a gin rummy game in Darlington, South Carolina, in 1949. He asked Sherman Ramsey, who owned a plot of land outside town, "Why don't we build a racetrack?" Ramsey didn't specifically say no, and the next week Brasington began pushing dirt around to build what he rather grandiosely called "Darlington International Raceway."

The next year—on Labor Day of 1950—the first Southern 500 was run, and the face of racing changed forever.

Brasington's 1.25-mile egg-shaped track was the biggest paved racetrack in the United States outside of Indianapolis, and the Southern 500 became the cornerstone of stock-car racing.

"We really enjoyed Darlington," said Hall of Fame car owner Bud Moore, who had an entry in the first Southern 500. "It was something new. All we had ever run was dirt. To come run a paved mile-and-a-quarter racetrack, it was something else. It was something to see 75 cars, three abreast, 25 rows."

Most Significant Tracks on the NASCAR Nextel Cup Schedule*

1. Daytona International Speedway (Daytona Beach, Florida). "The World Center of Racing" is the sport's mother church. A Daytona 500 victory is a signature achievement on any driver's résumé.
2. Darlington Raceway (Darlington, South Carolina). The first great racetrack for stock cars, Darlington still may offer the most complete test of a driver's ability.
3. Lowe's Motor Speedway (Concord, North Carolina). Most Nextel Cup teams are based in or around the Charlotte area, so this is their home turf. It's the template for the modern-day track.
4. Martinsville Speedway (Martinsville, Virginia). Racing at Martinsville is as retro as it gets these days, but the track has kept up with the sport's growth.
5. Indianapolis Motor Speedway (Indianapolis, Indiana). The most significant racing venue in America. When NASCAR became part of its story in 1994, stock car racing got a major boost.
6. Michigan International Speedway (Brooklyn, Michigan). The track closest to the automobile companies' Detroit headquarters has always had a role in keeping the factories interested and involved.
7. Richmond International Raceway (Richmond, Virginia). The track has been reshaped and reworked, but racers have been running in the Virginia capital almost since the Civil War cannons stopped echoing.
8. Talladega Superspeedway (Talladega, Alabama). When Bobby Allison's car nearly flew into the crowd in 1987, NASCAR figured out it had a speed limit and that 210 mph laps were beyond it.
9. Bristol Motor Speedway (Bristol, Tennessee). If you want to say you've seen all of America's truly great sports venues, you have to see Bristol. The atmosphere for the August night race is simply electric.
10. Texas Motor Speedway (Fort Worth, Texas). NASCAR moved toward bigger markets in the 1990s, and this is where that migration has put down the sturdiest roots.

* Ranking based on their historical, financial, and competitive impact on the sport.

That's how many cars started the first Southern 500, and in addition to being run on the biggest track the racers or fans had ever seen, part of the reason for the success of the first Southern 500 was the distance. Most stock car races up to then were 100- or maybe 200-lap affairs run around quarter- or half-mile dirt tracks.

In truth, no one knew if a showroom stock car could last for 500 miles on a big paved track in the heat of a late-summer South Carolina day. Nobody was sure the drivers could make it, either, for that matter. For the record, only 28 did, but the sheer spectacle of it all kicked racing up to a level it had never known.

It took six and a half hours and hundreds of tires, but at the end of it, a Californian Indy car driver named Johnny Mantz ushered in a new era.

Driving a little black showroom stock Plymouth, Mantz puttered around for 500 miles on one set of hard "Indy car" tires while the big dogs in their Lincolns, Cadillacs, and Buicks ate up a season's worth of rubber. Some teams resorted to "borrowing" tires off cars that had been driven to the track by paying customers, just to get through the long day.

Mantz finished nine laps ahead of Fireball Roberts's big Oldsmobile at an average speed of just over 75 mph.

Because of its unique shape, Darlington required a particular blend of skill and bravery. Before the track was reworked in 1969, drivers were required to "kiss" the outside wall off Turn 4 to get the most out of a lap.

"It was absolutely nerve-wracking," Cale Yarborough, the first five-time Southern 500 winner, said. "And you had to touch it every lap if you wanted to be fast. The trick was in knowing how hard to hit it [and] not to tear up your car."

For 10 years, Darlington International Raceway was *the* track, and the Southern 500 was *the* race. But that first Labor Day also planted a seed in the mind of France, NASCAR's founding father who'd put down his roots in Daytona Beach. France got his start in the racing business promoting events on the road and beach course used there. He dreamed of a track on which he could put his own stamp, and Daytona International Speedway became just that.

A sellout crowd watches the action at the 2001 Daytona 500 at the historic Daytona International Speedway, which one driver predicted upon its unveiling in 1959 would "separate the brave from the weak after the boys are gone."

DID YOU KNOW . . .
There was only one hotel in Darlington in 1950, so Bill France stayed at Harold Brasington's house for the first Southern 500? Harold Jr., all of nine years old, was in awe of "Big Bill," but never more so than when France asked him to get Joe DiMaggio on the phone.

In those days, connections were made by operators rather than dialing, so when little Harold told the operator he would like to speak to Joe DiMaggio, she said, "Honey, so would I," and hung up. But Junior was persistent, the call finally went through, and France conducted his business with the Yankee Clipper.

"Then," said Harold Jr., "I brought all my friends around to the house and told them, 'Joe DiMaggio talked on that phone.'"

When he completed it in 1959, it was twice as big as Darlington, 2.5 miles around. But with banked turns three stories high, it was capable of holding cars as fast as the mechanics could build them.

If the drivers were astounded at the first sight of Darlington, in Daytona they were awestruck. Driver Jimmy Thompson put it most succinctly. "There have been other tracks that separated the men from the boys," he said. "This is the track that will separate the brave from the weak after the boys are gone."

The finish of the first Daytona 500 on February 22, 1959, made it an instant classic. Johnny Beauchamp and Lee Petty went three wide with the lapped car of Joe Weatherly at the checkered flag. Beauchamp was declared the unofficial winner, but on the Wednesday following the Sunday race—after reviewing film footage shot by "Hearst Metrotone News of the Week"—NASCAR reversed itself and gave the trophy to Petty.

Later, Petty recalled his experience.

"I'll tell you what, there wasn't a man there who wasn't scared to death of the place," he said. "We never had raced on a track like that before. Darlington was big, but it wasn't banked like Daytona. What it amounted to was that we were all rookies going 30 to 40 miles per hour faster than we had ever gone before. There were some scared cats out there."

It took nearly 10 years for France and NASCAR to take the next step forward after Brasington turned a peanut patch into one of the hallowed halls of racing. But France's wildly successful new track spawned a spate of what people began calling "superspeedways," tracks longer than a mile, and racing again took a giant leap.

By the end of the century, there were only three oval tracks on NASCAR's elite Nextel Cup Series that were shorter than a mile. And with the rash of cookie-cutter tracks that were built afterward, more with sightlines and seating in mind, there will never be two more with the significance of the first two big ones.—J.M.

Second to None

Ask a race fan who was the best stock car racer who ever lived.

Before the fight starts, the argument usually breaks down predictably. The real old guys will scrap with you over whether it was Glenn "Fireball" Roberts or Curtis Turner. Newer fans will throw down over Dale Earnhardt or Jeff Gordon.

Now ask the people who followed racing during its real heyday, in the 1960s and '70s, when NASCAR grew out of the "bullring" era and into the superspeedway era, when racers still plied their trade on asphalt *and* dirt. For them, the field whittles down pretty quickly to two men: Richard Petty and David Pearson. A majority will go with Petty, since his 200 wins dwarf the rest. The others will say that there never lived a driver better than Pearson, known as the "Silver Fox."

That may be true.

Even though Petty's win total was nearly double that of Pearson's 105 and the total number of championships among the two (seven for Petty, three for Pearson) was more than double, on a pure pound-for-pound, race-for-race basis, Pearson was easily Petty's equal, and maybe a little better.

For Cotton Owens, the man who owned the team for which Pearson won the Grand National championship in 1966, there's no question.

"Believe me, I have seen a lot of great drivers, but I have never seen a driver who could outdrive David Pearson," Owens said. "He could go anywhere, anytime and could sit up front on a racetrack he'd never seen before. He just had that natural driving ability."

SEASON TO REMEMBER

David Pearson—1966

The pairing of legendary car owner Cotton Owens and David Pearson was hard to beat in 1966. Pearson won 15 races and seven poles in 42 starts, with 10 of his victories coming on dirt tracks, and finished in the top 10 33 times on his way to his first career NASCAR championship. Owens and Pearson parted ways the following year, but not before Pearson had scored 29 career victories in the car owner's Dodges.

Ask Petty, whose 35-year career overlapped the pioneers and the Johnny-come-latelys of the '80s and '90s, who was the best driver he ever raced against, and he never wavers. It's David Pearson.

Stock Car Racing Magazine (March 1993) printed, "David and I ran more firsts and seconds than anybody else, and we raced together on dirt tracks, superspeedways, road courses, big tracks, and little tracks," Petty said. "It didn't make any difference, you had to beat him every week."

That was true enough. From 1963 to 1977, the two finished first and second to each other 63 times. Pearson won 33, Petty, 30.

But the problem with making a comparison between the two is that Pearson wasn't there every week. In his career, Pearson drove only four full seasons. In three of those years (1966, 1968, and 1969), he won championships.

And while Petty drove every year but two for the powerhouse Petty Enterprises team, many of the seasons on either end of Pearson's career were spent running a handful of races in inferior equipment.

Pearson won his first championship driving for Owens, winning 15 of 42 races in 1966. Driving for the powerful Holman-Moody Ford "factory team" in 1968 and 1969, Pearson won 16 of 48 and 11 of 51, respectively.

Pole positions? Nobody was better. Pearson sat on the pole for 113 of 574 starts. At Charlotte (now Lowe's) Motor Speedway, he won 11 consecutive poles from 1973 to 1978.

SEASON TO REMEMBER

David Pearson—1968–69

When John Holman and Ralph Moody decided to show their Ford factory–backed superteam could win championships if that's what they chose to do, it was David Pearson who drove that point home for them. Pearson joined the Charlotte-based team in the middle of the 1967 season. In 1968, he won 16 races and 12 poles. He didn't do too badly the next year, either, winning 11 times with 44 top-10 finishes in 51 races. Oh, and he won the championship both years.

It is an oddity that Pearson never won a championship while driving for the famous Wood Brothers (1972–79) because they made a devastating team, but the Woods never raced a full season during that period. What Pearson did do when he was with the Woods, though, was win.

NASCAR had trimmed its schedule back to just 28 races in 1973, but Pearson and his team only ran the ones that paid the bigger purses. He ran only 18 times, but he won 11 of those. Pearson won five straight times that he raced in the spring, then after finishing second to Buddy Baker in the World 600 at Charlotte, he won his next four starts. Pearson ran 5,338 total laps that year and led for 2,658 of them.

It was during that era that the Petty-Pearson rivalry flourished, and the two put on some of the most thrilling races in history. One of the most famous finishes in NASCAR history was their last-lap duel in the 1976 Daytona 500, when both crashed coming off the final turn. Even while he was still sliding, Pearson came over his team's radio to ask, "Where's Richard? Where's Richard?"

Pearson kept his car running just enough to putter across the finish line at 30 mph while Petty's car sat smoldering in the trioval grass.

During a visit to the Wood Brothers shop in 2000, Len Wood, who was on the radio that day, let the world know exactly what the first words out of Pearson's mouth were: "He said, 'The bitch hit me!'" Wood said.

A couple of years before that, in the 1974 Firecracker 400, Pearson really made his bones. In those days before the carburetor restrictor plates, the preferred spot was second, where a driver could pull out and "slingshot" by the leader. Pearson, however, was in the lead. He had tried to tease Petty into passing him, but Petty was not falling for it.

So on the final lap, Pearson completely let off the accelerator, leaving Petty the option of running him over or passing him. When Petty flew by, Pearson tracked him down and passed him coming off

David Pearson shoulders his trophy in Victory Lane after winning the Southern 500 stock car race at Darlington Raceway in 1976, in which he became the first two-time winner of the Driver of the Year Award.

The King versus the Silver Fox

Richard Petty and David Pearson had perhaps the greatest rivalry in NASCAR history, sharing the track for parts of 27 seasons. They competed in the same race 550 times, and here's how they fared in relation to each other:

	Petty	Pearson
Head-to-head*	289	261
Wins	107	97
Top-five finishes	291	289
Top-10 finishes	366	349
Average finish	9.8	11.2

* Petty finished ahead of Pearson 289 times and Pearson finished ahead of Petty 261.

Source: www.racing-reference.info

the final turn. Pearson trusted Petty implicitly and knew that he was maybe the only other driver good enough to not wreck both of them. It was a move so audacious that had the situation been reversed, only Petty might have tried it.

Might is the key word. We'll never know if Petty would've. We only know that Pearson did.

The difference between Pearson and the competition, though, was not boldness and audacity. There were many with those qualities who sat on the sidelines with wrecked cars at the end of races. Pearson's gift was that he was better than anyone else at knowing exactly what was going on around him, and exactly what to do to take advantage of it.

Early in his career, some scientists checked the heart rates of selected drivers during races. Their findings showed that Pearson's heart rate during moments of extreme stress actually slowed down. No one was a better master of the moment.

Of all the remarkable numbers Pearson put up in his career the most remarkable one may be zero. That's the number of broken bones, number of visits to hospitals, and number of rides in track ambulances he had.

Not that he didn't have the chance. Once after a particularly savage crash at Bristol, Tennessee, Pearson looked down to see his shoes had been knocked off. Pearson knew an old wives' tale about people who had been killed in accidents coming separated from their footwear.

"I looked down there and I didn't know whether I was dead or not," he said. "When you die, you don't know whether you know what's going on or not. I couldn't wait until somebody came up and talked to me, to see if they'd answer me back."—J.M.

Smoke and Dollars

If you want to know why NASCAR is so successful, ask Junior Johnson. It was his foresight that gave the impetus to one of the biggest business/sports success story of the 20th century.

In 1971, NASCAR racing was still a struggling sport that had beaten back an attempt to unionize its drivers and had overcome a driver boycott at its biggest track two years earlier. But NASCAR may not have been capable of handling what happened that year. The American automobile manufacturers that had pumped lifeblood into the sport—either under or over the table—decided to withdraw their support.

A manufacturers' boycott had been a tool for a decade; when Ford thought it was getting the short shrift by NASCAR giving Chrysler an edge, it pulled out, and vice versa. But in 1971, the withdrawal was complete, and it looked permanent.

At that time, there were no big-bucks sponsors; most of a race teams' operating budgets—in cash and/or equipment—was furnished by the car makers. But in 1971, Chrysler said it would reduce from six factory-supported teams to two. Ford completely pulled out. General Motors had not been a serious player for years.

Then, when things looked gloomier than they had in a long time, a savior arrived.

Similar dark clouds had been hovering over the tobacco industry. With growing concerns over the effects of tobacco on health, in 1971 Congress pulled the plug on tobacco's lifeblood: TV advertising.

Two weeks after the Ford pullout from NASCAR, R.J. Reynolds Tobacco, through its Winston brand, announced that it would sponsor a race called the Winston 500 at Talladega, and set up a special point fund worth $100,000.

IF ONLY ...

T. Wayne Robertson had not died in a boating accident in 1998. At the time of his death, the R.J. Reynolds executive was rumored to be the man to lead racing into the next century—one way or the other.

The two most powerful men in racing, NASCAR president Bill France Jr. and Speedway Motorsports, Inc. chief Bruton Smith, both coveted Robertson's services. France was on the verge of retirement and needed a replacement. The timing would also have been perfect for Smith, France's rival. For years, he'd chafed under NASCAR's thumb (chafed quite well, mind you), but probably knew he didn't have the time or energy to engage in a massive battle for control of the sport.

Could Robertson have become the leader of a new racing series that would unseat NASCAR, or would he have been France's man? Either way, it would have been interesting.

All of this didn't happen in two weeks, of course. That's where Johnson comes into the story. Before the factory pullout, he drove across the state of North Carolina from his home in Wilkes County to Winston-Salem, seeking sponsorship. RJR had more than enough money to sponsor a race team, but it wasn't all that interested until the TV ban became a probability. When it became a reality, the tobacco companies had tons of money to spend in their advertising budgets with nowhere to spend it.

When Johnson realized just how much money there was on the table, he made the suggestion to RJR executives—why don't you sponsor racing? To that point, NASCAR's premier series had never had a "title" sponsor. But that changed with RJR's entry, and what had started as the Strictly Stock series in 1949 became the Winston Cup.

It was a marketing match made in heaven. RJR reasoned that the NASCAR fan base were some of the same people who smoked. If just NASCAR fans could be convinced to smoke Winstons, it would be almost a direct application of advertising dollars to its most likely customers. For NASCAR, it was money coming in that would reduce its dependence on the car makers.

Over the next 30 years, Winston Cup racing became the most popular form of motorsports in the country, and that $100,000 investment in that first race at Talladega grew into millions. But it

NASCAR's premiere series has changed names several times since 1949?

It began as the Strictly Stock series, a name used to describe the cars that were sometimes driven right off showroom floors with only the most basic modifications—taped-up headlights and beefed-up lug nuts, for instance.

The next season, the name was changed to the Grand National Series. In 1971, when R.J. Reynolds began its sponsorship, it officially became the Winston Cup Grand National Division, but many still called it Grand National until 1986.

That's when things really got confusing.

NASCAR dropped "Grand National" from the title, leaving it named Winston Cup, and passed that name along to the number two series. Once Anheuser-Busch bought title sponsorship of that, it became the Busch Grand National Series and is now known simply as the Busch Series.

The Winston Cup name remained until 2004 when Nextel took over as title sponsor of the number one series and the name became the Nextel Cup. Nextel merged with Sprint shortly thereafter and there was talk that another name change would be coming, but as of late 2006, the plan was to leave the Nextel brand on the series at least for the 2007 season.

wasn't a matter of just throwing money at a project. NASCAR had a good product. RJR showed them how to promote it. From the beginning, RJR supported racing from the ground up, everything from giving thousands of gallons of Winston's trademark red and white paint to spruce up hundreds of racetracks, to providing point funds for smaller series, to putting real money into a championship chest.

But the company made its biggest impact by promoting racing like no one had ever done, and most of the credit for that should go to two men—Ralph Seagraves and T. Wayne Robertson.

Seagraves was a district manager for RJR in Washington, D.C., when the deal was cut. He was a politician of the first degree who also happened to be a huge race fan, a larger-than-life figure who moved easily in the halls of power—both in government and in business. Seagraves's approach was different. He wasn't out to sell cigarettes. Sell racing, he said, and cigarettes will go along for the ride.

"Ralph was the perfect man for the time," said Jeff Byrd, who worked with both Seagraves and Robertson in RJR's marketing department. "Just as T. Wayne was perfect for his time, when he took over after Ralph retired in 1984."

In the beginning, racing and RJR needed a backslapper who could be an arm-twister, which defined Seagraves perfectly. As the business grew bigger, it needed a more sophisticated approach to basically the same job, and Robertson was an ideal fit for that.

Both men moved with ease in both the garage and the board-room, with the ability to identify problems at the grassroots level and solve them, and to convince RJR to spend ever-increasing amounts of money on the sport.

For instance, in 1989, when RJR-Nabisco was bought out by Kohlberg Kravis Roberts & Co., that lifeblood was under threat. Robertson, a guy with only a two-year tech school degree, went up against the KKR power brokers in an attempt to keep the Winston Cup program alive.

"He didn't just keep the program going," Byrd said. "When it was all over, Wayne had more people and more money."

Winston's involvement led to other nonautomotive companies' involvement in the sport, due in no small measure to both Seagraves and Robertson. At the time of the death of both men—notably, both in 1998—Fortune 500 companies as team sponsors were the norm rather than the exception.

But in 2003, RJR and other major tobacco companies reached a "master settlement agreement" with several states' attorneys general to settle lawsuits against them. While that agreement included provisions that would allow RJR to continue its NASCAR sponsorship, both NASCAR and the tobacco company agreed that if another primary sponsor could be found for the sport's top series RJR would withdraw.

In short order, the Winston Cup became the Nextel Cup, and racing, for better or worse, had changed dance partners. Whether a communications company such as Nextel will be able to carry the momentum built by Winston for another 30 years is a matter for debate.

One thing is for certain: it will never be the same.—J.M

Buck and Buddy

The first automobile race Buck Baker saw was at a track in Greensboro, North Carolina. Buck, who'd just come out of the navy, went with a group of his buddies. Just as the feature was beginning, Buck got up to leave.

One of his pals asked where he was going. "I'm leaving," Buck said. "They're not doing anything I can't do."

Buck Baker then spent a racing career proving he knew exactly what he was talking about.

Elzie Wylie "Buck" Baker drove in the first race ever held in what's now the NASCAR Nextel Cup Series in 1949 in Charlotte, North Carolina, the town where he'd worked as a bus driver. By the time he drove his final race at Charlotte Motor Speedway in October 1976, Buck had been in 637 races and had won 46.

He also helped his son, Buddy, start his own racing career.

Buck and Buddy Baker, in many respects, could not be more different. You could use words like "irascible" and "cantankerous" to accurately describe Buck. Buddy, on the other hand, is one of the most affable men to ever drive a race car. But when it came to racing, it was most definitely like father, like son. Both tried their dead-level best to wring every ounce of speed out of every car they ever sat in.

Buck Baker also lived about as hard as he drove. NASCAR founder Bill France Sr. once joked that every year before racers came to Daytona he'd go down to the jail and give the sheriff some money for Baker's bail. That way, France said, he saved himself a call in the middle of the night that was almost bound to be coming.

Buck, who died in 2002, was once driving a bus with about a dozen passengers on board from Charlotte down to Columbia, South

SEASON TO REMEMBER

Buck Baker—1956

Mercurial car owner Carl Kiekhaefer had won a championship with Tim Flock in 1955, but the next year Flock left the team after running just eight races. Kiekhaefer kept right on clicking, however, with Buck Baker roaring to the first of his two championships with 14 victories and 12 poles in 44 races in Kiekhaefer's cars. Baker finished in the top 10 in 39 of the total of 48 races he entered that season.

Carolina. They passed a brightly lit dance hall on the road in between, and depending on which version of the story you believe, either Baker or the passengers decided they wanted to stop. A few hours later, everybody on the bus was passed out drunk, and everybody in Columbia was wondering what had happened to it.

When Buddy was just a boy, he and his parents were heading to Florence, South Carolina, to see some relatives. Buck was driving an Oldsmobile he'd bought with plans to turn it into a race car. Baker's mother, Margaret, was driving a Cadillac, and Buddy was riding with her. Buck pulled out to pass her on the highway. Margaret immediately returned the favor, but knowing her husband she started to back off.

"Me, being the little competitive fool that I was, I jumped down in the floorboard and held her foot down on the accelerator," Buddy said. "We went by the yard where my grandmother and all the uncles and aunts were sitting around. I reached up and blew the horn to make sure everybody saw us.... Dad was mad. We were there all weekend and he never spoke to a soul."

Buddy made his racing debut in April of 1959 on a half-mile dirt track in Columbia. He remembers it vividly. "I was all over the racetrack and I was blaming the car," he said. "I said, 'This is the biggest piece of junk I ever sat down in.' But Dad's car blew up and he motioned for me to come in. I got out and he got in that same car and made up two or three of the laps I was behind. I said, 'I've got some stuff to learn.'"

Buck and Buddy appeared in the same race 187 times in NASCAR's top series. Buck won three of those races and finished ahead of his son 102 times.

Both of them seemed to have a little trouble "coming down" after big victories. After one of the three times he won the Southern 500 at Darlington Raceway, Buck got a speeding ticket in one of the small towns between the South Carolina track and Charlotte.

"The officer was lecturing Buck about how he, of all people, should know how dangerous speed could be," longtime motorsports writer Tom Higgins said. "Buck told the guy, 'Look, if you're going to give me a ticket, give it to me. If I hadn't been in a hurry, I wouldn't have been speeding.' The officer took him off to jail."

Buddy Baker often joked that he won the Daytona 450 a half-dozen times or more, but something would always happen to him in those final 50 miles to deny him a win in the sport's biggest race. Finally, in 1980, Baker won the Daytona 500—one of his 19 career victories in 699 Cup starts. Baker went back to his hotel after the postrace festivities, but he was way too keyed up to sleep. "I twisted and I turned and I finally said, 'This is stupid; I am going home,'" Buddy said. "I got up and got in the car to drive home. I was riding along listening to the radio—it was the middle of the night."

Just as he crossed from Florida into Georgia, Baker came over a rise in the road and his radar detector went off. The state trooper was sitting there in the edge of the woods. Baker didn't even wait for the trooper to come after him. He just pulled over, knowing he'd been busted.

DID YOU KNOW . . . In March 1970, Buddy Baker became the first man to drive a car at an officially timed average speed of more than 200 mph on a closed course? Baker drove a Dodge Daytona, a car with a tall aerodynamic wing on its rear, at Talladega Superspeedway and posted an official time of 200.447 mph. "I could have run 210 mph," Baker said years later. "We got a lot of attention for it. It wasn't really a big deal for me back then, but it became a big part of my life."

Buddy Baker is congratulated after his win in the 1975 Los Angeles Times 500 in Ontario, California.

The trooper pulled in behind Baker's car. "Buddy Baker," he said as he walked to the driver's window. "I am going to tell you, you are my favorite driver. I always pull for you. But you have the most rotten luck. And this is another example of that."

At least, Baker said, the officer gave him a break on the speed. "I have no idea how fast I was going," Baker admitted.

Buck and Buddy were both included when NASCAR named its 50 greatest drivers in 1998. Both are members of various racing halls of fame as well. But the greatest honor Buddy Baker said he ever received came the day he got his first Cup victory in the National 500 at Charlotte Motor Speedway.

Buck wasn't racing that day; he'd broken his leg in a wreck. After Buddy won, though, Buck made his way to victory lane to congratulate his son.

"Tears were running down his cheeks," Buddy said. "He put his hand around the back of my head and pulled me over to him and said, 'You know, you did almost as well as I could have done.' That was just him. That was like saying, 'Great job. I'm proud of you, son.'"—D.P.

SEASON TO REMEMBER

Richard Petty—1967

Buddy Baker's victory in the National 500 at Charlotte Motor Speedway in October 1967 was a breakthrough not only for Baker, who got his first career win that day, but also for the rest of NASCAR's best. Baker became the first driver other than Richard Petty to win a race in more than two months. On August 12, Petty won at Bowman Gray Stadium in Winston-Salem to start an all-time record streak of 10 straight victories. He won 27 races that year, another record that will almost certainly never be broken, and finished in the top five 38 times in 48 races. He also won 18 poles and, as you might guess, the championship.

Triumph and Tragedy

Few families in racing ever achieved the heights of the Allisons. No family ever paid a higher price for glory.

Bobby Allison, whose 85 victories in NASCAR's Nextel Cup Series is third on the all-time win list, was the 1983 champion. But his career—and very nearly his life—ended with a wreck at Pocono, Pennsylvania, in 1988.

Bobby's kid brother Donnie won 10 races in NASCAR's premier series, and finished fourth as a rookie in the Indianapolis 500 in 1970, a week after winning the World 600 in Charlotte. His career was shortened by a savage wreck at Charlotte in 1981. He only drove 13 races after the crash.

Clifford Allison, Bobby's youngest son, died before his racing career had a chance to bloom, in a wreck in a Busch Series car during practice at Michigan International Speedway in 1992.

Davey Allison, Bobby's oldest son who may have been the best driver of the lot, died when his helicopter crashed in the infield at Talladega Superspeedway 11 months to the day after Clifford Allison died. At the time of his death, Davey had 19 Winston Cup wins and had finished third in the championship standings twice.

The misery of losing two sons was so great that it drove Bobby and his wife, Judy, apart for a time. Clearly, of all the families in a family sport, the Allisons had more than their share of heartache.

"The voodoo was after us," Bobby once said. "But a long time ago my dad taught me to accept life as it came every day. That was my dad's one big lesson to me.

"You must do the best you can each day. If it's a good day, enjoy it, and do the best you can tomorrow. If it's a bad day, you accept it. And you do the best you can tomorrow."

Somehow, you'd expect no less from a member of the "Alabama Gang."

"A lot of people assume I was born in Alabama," Bobby Allison said. "But I was actually born in Miami."

So, too, were the Allison family's racing dreams. Bobby and his brother Donnie, who is two years younger, were born into a big family in that South Florida city and attended school there. Their grandfather, Arthur Patton, took them to all sorts of sporting events, and on one trip he took Bobby to one of the short tracks in the area.

Bobby thinks he might have been 10 years old. "From there on," he said, "all I could think about was racing."

Davey Allison (left) chats with his father, Bobby Allison, after a practice session at Pocono International Raceway in 1988.

Red Farmer, a slightly older friend who would go on to become one of the greatest short-track racers of all time, was racing at a one-third-mile track at Hialeah Speedway, and Bobby and Donnie began going there, too. They raced at a track at the Palm Beach County fairgrounds.

Bobby won an amateur division race at Hialeah and knew he wanted to keep at it. But his father wanted him to finish school, too, and Bobby did. After graduation, he went to Wisconsin, where he had a job at the proving grounds for Mercury's outboard boat motors, owned by millionaire Carl Kiekhaefer, who also owned several NASCAR race teams.

In the winter, Allison was part of the crew that moved to work in Sarasota, Florida. That allowed him to race at some of the tracks in Florida on the weekends, but the real eye-opener for Allison came when Kiekhaefer asked him to drive a car up to the race teams' shop in Charlotte, North Carolina.

"I saw that race shop and I said, 'Wow, this is the place for me,'" Bobby said.

One of the first people Allison met was the legendary mechanic Ray Fox, the teams' crew chief.

"Ray asked me, 'Are you a mechanic?'" Bobby explained. "I told him I was a good one. So we went back in the shop and he gave me a sheet of paper. It was an instruction sheet for preparing a car. He said, 'Get this car ready; you can use my tools.'

"A couple of hours later I went over to him and said, 'What's next?' He said, 'Are you done?' I said, 'Sure, your sheet told me what to do.' So he said, 'Boy, I've got to keep you here.' I was only at that shop for two months. But in the time I was there, I saw 19 races run out of that shop, and nobody else's car won a race."

Allison still wanted to drive, and when a friend who had been racing in Georgia told him he was planning to go try his luck on paved tracks in Alabama, Allison, using $100 he'd won in a race in West Palm Beach, decided that sounded like a good idea.

Bobby and Donnie hooked a trailer carrying their modified car to a truck and set off for Alabama. When they got there, they thought they'd found a pot of gold. Bobby finished fifth in a heat and fifth in the feature one night. When it was over he went to the pay window

DID YOU KNOW . . .

Bobby Allison has one win that's not in the record books? NASCAR's official records list Bobby Allison and Darrell Waltrip both with 84 victories. But Allison contends he should be credited with 85, and most historians agree.

The controversy hinges on the Myers Brothers 250 at Bowman Gray Stadium in Winston-Salem, on August 6, 1971. With NASCAR needing cars to fill up fields in its Grand National Series, Allison was allowed to enter that race in a 1970 Ford Mustang, a car used in Grand American Series races. Allison won the race in that car, but because he was not in a Grand National car he was not credited with the win.

But if Allison didn't win the race, who did? Richard Petty finished second in a Grand National car, but he didn't get credit for the victory either. Officially, nobody did. In similar circumstances in other races, the driver who won in a non–Grand National car was credited with the win.

Historians and NASCAR officials met to discuss the controversy and, everyone thought, had agreed to change the records to give Allison the 85th win—and we have done that in this book. But officially, that still has not happened. So the controversy lives on.

expecting to get enough money for him and Donnie to get a hamburger and sleep in the truck. His prize, though, was $135. The next night at Montgomery, he finished second and won around $400. The next weekend, Bobby won his first feature at Montgomery.

"Alabama became home to me very quickly," he said. "There was just something about the people there; they were all just so nice to me."

The Allisons and Farmer came to be known as the "Alabama Gang" because they developed a habit of dropping in at tracks all over the Southeast and going home with the bulk of the money. Donnie once noted that other drivers hated seeing the Alabama Gang pull into the pits as much as bank tellers dreaded seeing the James Gang walk into their banks.

Bobby was clearly the more driven—some would say hotheaded—of the two brothers. It might be unfair to say he raced with a chip on his shoulder, but he was never better than when the odds were against him, which was often.

"The thing I think I might be most proud of is that I won Winston Cup races in eight different brands of cars—Chevrolet, Pontiac, Buick, Ford, Mercury, Plymouth, Dodge, and the AMC Matador," Bobby said. "Nobody else has come close to that."

Nobody else had to. Most drivers with that kind of success find good rides with major teams and stay there. But Allison frequently found himself at odds with NASCAR, with team owners, and with fellow drivers because of his unflinching belief in what he felt was right.

Allison got his first career win at Oxford, Maine, in 1966 in a car owned by J.D. Bracken. He went on to win in cars owned by Cotton Owens, Holman-Moody, Tom Friedkin, Mario Rossi, Melvin Joseph, Richard Howard, Junior Johnson, Roger Penske, Bud Moore, Harry Ranier, DiGard, the Stavola Brothers, and of course, Bobby Allison.

Perhaps the most pivotal season in Allison's career was 1972, when he won 10 of 31 races and finished second in 12 more while driving for Johnson. Johnson and Allison were a pair of headstrong mules who won despite pulling in opposite directions, and they lasted only one season as a team. Many years later, Johnson noted that if they had stayed together, it would have been Bobby with 200 career wins and not Richard Petty.

The 1972 season also saw a fierce feud develop between the Allisons and Petty, and they slammed and banged each other from one end of the country to the other. It was the same a few years later with Darrell Waltrip.

Then there was The Fight.

In 1979, CBS televised the Daytona 500 live from start to finish for the first time ever, and it would have been exciting enough on its own merits. But the Allison brothers and Cale Yarborough piqued the interest of a nationwide audience.

Donnie and Cale were battling for the win when they tangled and crashed on the final lap. Richard Petty sailed by to get the win, but that was quickly overshadowed when TV commentator Ken Squier shouted, "There's a fight!"

Cale and Donnie had a brief shouting match after they climbed from their wrecked cars, but according to Donnie, that was largely over by the time Bobby arrived to check on his brother.

Bobby said he just wanted to check to make sure Donnie was all right.

"But Cale started to yell at me, and I think I might have questioned his ancestry," Bobby said. "He ran at me and more words went back and forth. He ran to my car and he hit me in the face with his helmet."

Bobby said he saw a couple of drops of his blood on the leg of his uniform. He was still in his car at the time, but he said he knew he had to get out and confront Yarborough or "I'd be running from him the rest of my life."

And then the darndest thing happened.

"I got out of the car," Bobby said, "and Cale went to beating on my fist with his nose."

Regardless of who started it or who got in the last lick, the raw emotions of racing were laid bare for the whole world to see. NASCAR, to put it mildly, took a giant leap forward.

But if there were bad moments, the Allison clan never had a sweeter one than in the 1988 Daytona 500. In his brief career, Davey

TOP 9

Brothers Who Each Won in NASCAR's Top Series*

1.	Bobby and Donnie Allison	95
2.	Darrell and Michael Waltrip	88
3.	Tim, Bob, and Fonty Flock	62
4.	Herb and Donald Thomas	49
5.	Terry and Bobby Labonte**	43
6.	Jeff and Ward Burton	22
	Benny and Phil Parsons	22†
8.	Geoffrey and Brett Bodine	19
9.	Kurt and Kyle Busch	18

* As of September 22, 2006.

** The Labontes are the only brothers to both win championships.

Source: www.racing-reference.info

DID YOU KNOW . . . Like his father, Davey Allison suffered serious injuries in a crash at Pocono Raceway? In July 1992, Allison's No. 28 Ford had been strong through the first portion of the race and looked like the car to beat. But on Lap 149, Allison and Darrell Waltrip made contact in the Pocono track's "tunnel turn" and Allison's car went into the grass. After several violent barrel rolls, it would up upside-down with Allison still inside.

Allison suffered a broken arm and wrist, a concussion, and numerous bruises. But because he was still in the championship race, a determined Allison and his team spent the week before the next race figuring out a way for the battered driver to start the race.

Allison spent the week in the hospital, but he made it to the track to practice in the car enough for NASCAR to approve of his starting the race. Under Cup rules, points for a car's finish go to the driver who takes the green flag.

Allison's hand had to be attached to the gearshift knob using Velcro, but he still managed to drive the No. 28 to an early caution flag. At that point, Bobby Hillin got in the car and Allison got out. Hillin drove to a third-place finish that helped keep the team's championship hopes alive.

had shown flashes of the same brilliance his dad possessed. That day he was never better, but there was one man capable of outshining him.

Bobby and Davey, in that order, raced for the checkered flag, separated by only a couple of car lengths. No chicanery, no blocking. Just racing.

"My whole career, I've done my best to play it straight," Bobby said later, a beaming Davey by his side. "And when you are racing against the best youngster to ever come along, you wouldn't want to do anything other than that."

If the torch was not passed that day, it was lit. Tragically, for the entire Allison clan, it would never come to full flame.

Davey Allison made his Cup debut at Talladega, the Alabama track that became home turf for the family, in 1985 and finished 10th. Davey got his first career victory at Talladega two years later, in a car owned by Ranier.

Just a few months after their 1-2 finish in the Daytona 500 in 1988, Bobby wrecked violently in the Miller High Life 500 at Pocono.

TOP 10

Drivers with the Most Career Starts in NASCAR's Top Series*

1.	Richard Petty	1,185
2.	Dave Marcis	883
3.	Ricky Rudd	875
4.	Terry Labonte	845
5.	Darrell Waltrip	809
6.	Kyle Petty	776
7.	Bill Elliott	752
8.	Bobby Allison	719
9.	Rusty Wallace	706
10.	Sterling Marlin	702

* As of September 22, 2006.

Source: NASCAR Statistical Services

A tire went down and Allison spun into the grass and then back across into the outside wall. His car slid across the track again and was hit in the door by the car driven by Jocko Maggiacomo.

An emergency worker climbed into Bobby's mangled car and performed a tracheotomy. It took nearly 45 minutes—with Davey passing the scene of his father's wreck as cars continued around the track—for Bobby to be cut free and taken to the hospital. He was unconscious for four days and spent more than a hundred days in hospitals beginning his recovery. He spent months in almost constant pain and working through therapy in which he had to relearn many of life's most basic skills. There are parts of his memory that have never come back.

Davey Allison picked up the family's mantel and was carrying it brilliantly. In 1998 engine builder Robert Yates bought the team from Ranier, and Davey became one of the sport's most popular young stars. By late in the 1992 season, he had won 18 points races, had scored back-to-back victories in the sport's all-star race, and was in contention to win the championship in a dramatic battle with Alan Kulwicki and Bill Elliott. But a crash in the final race at Atlanta left him third in the standings for a second straight year.

Earlier that summer, tragedy struck the Allison family when Clifford was killed in a crash during a Busch Series practice at Michigan Speedway.

Davey got his 19th career win at Richmond in the third race of the 1993 season. That August, however, he was flying a helicopter into the infield at Talladega when the chopper crashed violently. Red Farmer was pulled from the wreckage, but Davey was badly injured. He died the next day.

"The sport has, I guess, been a mixed blessing for me," Bobby Allison said, looking back on a career and life that are among the most distinguished as well as the most anguish-ridden in NASCAR's history. "There have been some really good times and some really bad times. But I know that there are other people who had the bad times but didn't get to have to the good ones, too."—J.M. and D.P.

Checks, Credit, and Cash

Pressure is relative.

Sure, when you're competing at the very highest level in any endeavor, expectations must be met or otherwise dealt with. If you're staring at a five-foot putt to win The Masters golf tournament or standing at the free-throw line with the NCAA basketball championship on the line, it's hard not to have a little bit of cotton mouth.

It could be easily argued, however, that it's far more difficult to compete when your very livelihood is on the line.

Like, for instance, the time in 1959 when Ned Jarrett needed a race car. A car owner had one that he was willing to let go of for $2,000, and that would have been fine except for one small detail: Jarrett didn't have $2,000.

He did, however, have a checkbook. So late on a Friday afternoon, he wrote a $2,000 check and purchased himself a race car. Then he went out and won two races that weekend and raced to the bank first thing Monday morning to deposit his winnings so the check would clear.

Now that's performing under pressure.

Since those early days, of course, stock car racing has been very good to the Jarrett family from Catawba County, North Carolina. Ned retired after winning 50 races and two championships at NASCAR's top level and then became one of the most respected and popular ambassadors for his sport in a long, distinguished career in broadcasting.

In that latter role, he had the remarkable privilege of being in the booth doing the national telecast of NASCAR's biggest race and

SEASON TO REMEMBER

Ned Jarrett—1965

Ned Jarrett won the NASCAR championship in 1961 and then won 15 races in 60 starts in 1964, but it was in 1965 where he enjoyed his most consistently outstanding year. Jarrett won 13 races on his way to another championship in 1965, including the prestigious Southern 500 at Darlington. He also won nine poles, but his most remarkable statistic was 42 top-five finishes in 54 races. Jarrett also finished second 13 times and third 10 more. For the season, his average finish was 4.9.

watching his son score an emotional Daytona 500 victory that is just one of the highlights of Dale Jarrett's own career.

But while Dale's father has been nothing but supportive of his son's racing exploits, the same cannot be said for Ned's father.

As a teenager, Ned worked alongside his dad, Homer, in the sawmill. But one of the most storied and historic short tracks in racing history, Hickory Motor Speedway, opened in 1952 near their home and Ned drove a car in its first race, finishing 10th.

Homer was a race fan, and he'd taken his son with him to see some races, but he didn't want his son driving a car. Working on them was fine, but no driving. And for a while, Ned obeyed his father's wishes and just worked on the car that he and his brother-in-law John Lentz owned.

But one night Lentz showed up very ill. He wasn't able to drive, but he had a plan. He and Ned looked enough alike that Ned could be his substitute. Ned put on the helmet and climbed into the car. Nobody knew the difference that night when Jarrett, posing as Lentz, finished second.

Jarrett and Lentz decided that Ned was the one who should be driving the car, so Ned kept doing it. But the ruse ended the night when the "wrong" John Lentz got his first win. When Jarrett climbed out of the car in victory lane, the charade was over. And in a town as small as Hickory, where the weekly races were a pretty big deal, it didn't take long for Homer to find out what his son had been up to.

Ned Jarrett's decision to retire as a driver at the age of 34 may have been influenced by the 1964 World 600 at Charlotte Motor Speedway?

On Lap 7 of that race, Jarrett and Junior Johnson wrecked between Turns 1 and 2. Fireball Roberts came off the second turn, saw the wreck, and spun his car to try to avoid the other two cars. But Roberts's No. 22 Ford rammed into an opening on the inside wall and flipped over onto its roof. Gasoline began leaking into the car with Roberts still strapped in it. Drivers didn't have fire-retardant suits in those days, but most of them wore suits that had been dipped into a fire-resistant solution. Roberts didn't even have that much protection—he had asthma and the chemical made it hard for him to breathe.

As Jarrett's car finally came to a stop, he saw that Roberts's car had burst into flames. He ran over to help his fellow driver, with Roberts yelling, "My God, Ned! Help me! I'm on fire!" Jarrett helped Roberts out of his car, but Roberts was burned over more than three-quarters of his body. Roberts, one of the sport's most popular figures, held on for nearly six weeks in a Charlotte hospital, but died on July 2. He is buried in a cemetery near Daytona International Speedway.

"He came to me and said, 'Ned, if you're going to race, you might as well be the one getting credit for it,'" Jarrett said.

From that day on, Jarrett made a name for himself. He won the track championship at Hickory in 1955, no small feat at that track where so many former and current stars have raced, then added NASCAR Sportsman series titles in 1957 and 1958.

When he came to the top-tier Grand National series the next year, the only two races he won were the two he needed to win to pay off the check for the car he'd bought. He won five times in 1960, then had only one win in 1961 but finished in the top 10 in 34 of the 46 races he entered and won his first championship.

By 1964 Jarrett was driving for car owner Bondy Long, and despite winning 15 races, he finished second in the standings to Richard Petty. But the next year Jarrett won 13 more races and his second championship.

His biggest victory in 1965, and the biggest of his career, came in the Southern 500 at Darlington. In a race where driver Buren

Skeen died from injuries suffered in an early wreck, and where Cale Yarborough flew over the guard rail right out of the track into the parking lot in another spectacular wreck, Jarrett was running third when Fred Lorenzen and Darel Dieringer both saw their motors give way. Jarrett inherited the lead and won by an amazing margin of 14 laps, the biggest winning margin in the history of the series.

But in 1966, with Jarrett in the running for another title, Ford announced yet another in a series of manufacturer pullouts that plagued the sport in that era. Jarrett, surprisingly, decided at that point he'd raced long enough. Twenty-one races into the season, the sport's reigning champion retired—at the age of 34.

He went back home to Hickory to raise his family and make a living, eventually promoting the races at the same track where he'd first raced. It would be more than a decade before he went to work as a broadcaster, working first for radio's Motor Racing Network and then for various television networks, including CBS at the Daytona 500.

Just before Ned began his broadcasting career, Dale realized he too wanted to be a driver. He'd played other sports in high school quite well (Jarrett was offered but elected not to take a scholarship to play golf in college), and found it much easier to just show up at football or golf practice than to get somebody to help him get started in racing.

Finally, he and two high school buddies, Andy Petree and Jimmy Newsome, started building a race car. They still didn't have an engine, or the $2,500 it would take to get one. But Ned's connections helped out there, and because his father had come through with the missing piece of the equation, Dale was elected as the team's driver.

When the car was finally ready, there wasn't time for any practice. The fledgling team didn't make qualifying, either. But they were there for the race. Jarrett had driven on the track by himself before, but until he lined up last in a 24-car field for his first green flag, he had never been on a track with another car.

Jarrett did not win. But Ned tells the story that 1970 Winston Cup champion Bobby Isaac was there that night and knew that Dale was supposed to be in the car. When Dale started passing cars, Isaac

TOP 6

Father-Son Driver Tandems in NASCAR History

	Drivers	Total Wins
1.	Lee (50) and Richard Petty (200)	250
2.	Richard (200) and Kyle Petty (8)	208
3.	Bobby (85) and Davey Allison (19)	104
4.	Dale (76) and Dale Earnhardt Jr. (16)	92
5.	Ned (50) and Dale Jarrett (32)	82
6.	Buck (46) and Buddy Baker (19)	65

Source: NASCAR Statistical Services

found Ned and asked him why Dale wasn't driving. Ned said he was. Isaac couldn't believe how well Dale was doing for his first time out.

Inside the car, Dale couldn't believe how much fun he was having. When the race was over, he went bounding into the stands looking for his parents and, when he found them, said, "I found it! This is what I want to do."

"It was just unbelievable," Dale recalled. "I mean, I had no idea."

It's a good thing Dale found such a passion for racing; otherwise, he most likely would not have been able to endure the long road he took to get from that rough beginning to where he is today. Jarrett made it to the Busch Series by 1982, but it took him until his 131st race in that series to finally get a victory. He ran his first nearly full season in 1986 and went 128 races without a win there until his first win at Michigan in 1991.

Two years later, a remarkable thing happened in the Daytona 500. Jarrett was starting his second year with a team that Washington Redskins coach Joe Gibbs had started. His crew chief was Jimmy Makar, who also happened to be married to Dale's sister, Patti. Up in the CBS broadcast booth sat his father.

In the final laps of the 500, it came down to Dale versus Dale. Jarrett was racing the legendary Dale Earnhardt, who was still looking for his first Daytona 500 win, and with Ned being allowed by his colleagues to make a memorable last-lap call, Dale Jarrett won the race.

By the end of the 1994 season, Jarrett was preparing to start his own Cup team. But Ernie Irvan's crash at Michigan in the Robert Yates Racing Ford left Yates needing a driver for one year, since Irvan was determined to make it back into the car after his injuries healed. Jarrett figured he could learn a lot about running a team from Yates while driving fast race cars too, so he signed on for the 1995 season.

Irvan was back by the end of that year, but Yates decided to go to a two-car operation. He put Jarrett in a No. 88 Ford and paired him with crew chief Todd Parrott for the 1996 season. All they did was go out and win the Daytona 500—with Earnhardt finishing second again—and three more races.

Winston Cup champion Dale Jarrett is interviewed in his car on pit road by his father, Ned Jarrett, also a Winston Cup champion, as he prepares for the start of the NAPA 500 at Atlanta Motor Speedway in 1999.

Jarrett finished in the top five in the final standings each year for six seasons in the No. 88, winning 24 races and the 1999 championship in that span. He remained the driver of the No. 88 Fords until the end of the 2006 season. In 2007, he will join Michael Waltrip Racing to drive Toyotas in what he has said will be the first of his final two seasons of Cup competition.

Jarrett has already won over $55 million in his Cup career, but he still has the envelope in which he collected the money he won in that first race at Hickory 30 years ago. All $35 of it.—D.P.

Fare Thee Well, BP

It is ironic that 1973 Winston Cup champion Benny Parsons, a racing color commentator these days, will be forever known as the "Detroit Taxi Driver" who won racing's biggest prize. Parsons grew up about as far removed from Detroit as you can get.

A native of Wilkes County, North Carolina, Parsons was reared by his great-grandmother, "Mama Julia," in a little community called Parsonsville, on Rendezvous Ridge. His parents left Wilkes County seeking a better life after World War II, taking baby brother Phil with them. Benny didn't join his parents until after he graduated from high school.

"They couldn't afford to take both of us, so they left me with my great-grandmother, and by the time they got up there and got settled in, she'd gotten attached and they let me stay with her," Parsons said. "But I did drive a cab in Detroit, so I guess that will always stick with me."

Parsons spent more time working on them at his dad's cab company and garage than he did driving them, but that was where he got his start in racing. It was not difficult being a race fan, growing up near North Wilkesboro, but it was not until some buddies stopped by the garage in Detroit that he actually drove a race car. They were on their way to a local track and, that night, their regular driver didn't show up, so Parsons drove the car.

He was hooked. Parsons raced on the Midwest Automobile Racing Club of America circuit, winning national titles in 1968 and 1969. Then he returned to the little North Carolina town of Ellerbe, near the track in Rockingham, to become a full-time racer, often listing "taxicab driver" as his occupation on entry forms.

The thing people remember most about Parsons is the unusual way he won the Grand National championship in 1973. Many modern-day fans who know him only as a TV guy don't connect that with the fact that he was a great race car driver. But in fact, when he began racing for L.G. DeWitt (whom Parsons always referred to as "Mr. DeWitt") in 1970, he finished no lower than 11th in the championship race in the 12 seasons in which he drove full-time.

He drove DeWitt's cars from 1970 to 1978, then drove two seasons for M.C. Anderson and one for Bud Moore before reducing his schedule in 1982. He finished his career driving for Johnny Hayes, Richard and Leo Jackson, and Hendrick Motorsports, driving his final season for old-timer Junie Donlavey in 1988. He finished his racing career with 21 victories, which included the 1975 Daytona 500, the 1978 Rebel 500 at Darlington, the 1980 Gabriel 400 at Michigan International Speedway, and the 1984 Coca-Cola 500 at Atlanta.

TRIVIA

Parsons was always a favorite with the racing press because he gave thoughtful answers, and the gift of gab served him well once he hung up his helmet. He worked as a color man on both radio and TV after his racing days, and as of the 2006 season, he had worked with NBC/TNT for six years and had his own radio show on the Performance Racing Network, "Fast Talk," for a dozen years.

"I love the people involved in racing, and the fact that I can still continue to be a part of it is fantastic," Parsons said.

The way Parsons won the championship in 1973 is worth retelling, because it not only says a lot about the way racing was back then, but also a lot more about the kind of man Parsons was.

Parsons entered the final race of the season, the American 500 at Rockingham, with a 194.35-point lead over Richard Petty in the championship chase. The way the points were structured then, the number of laps completed was as important as where you finished.

"It was amazing," Parsons said. "The race had begun, and I was in the perfect spot. I was about fifth or sixth, and didn't have much

The "Detroit Taxi Driver," Benny Parsons, goes through the "S" Turn at Riverside International Raceway in 1978.

traffic. I was basically in a straightaway by myself. I thought, 'Wouldn't it be perfect to run like this all day?'"

That plan went out the window on the 13th lap. Parsons came through the second turn when he saw the car driven by Johnny Barnes sitting dead ahead.

"I hit him," Parsons said. "We didn't have spotters, and the caution flag came out after I'd gone by. I was going around the corner blind and there he sat in the middle of the racetrack." Parsons refired his car, but it would not move. Then, he said, for some reason he looked over to his right. "I could not believe what I saw," he said. "There was no right side, none at all."

He got back to his pit, but his hopes for a championship were dashed. So he thought. As he and his crew chief, Travis Carter, were surveying the damage, something remarkable happened. Members of other teams came over to see if they could help.

"There were several people who came down and said, 'Whatever we can do, holler at us,'" he said. "Today, teams are self-sufficient. But in 1973 they weren't. They went and got pieces and brought them back—whatever we needed. We told them, and they'd do it. They got it from other teams."

Incredibly, Parsons was able to return to the race 136 laps after the wreck. He puttered around the rest of the way, finishing 308

TRIVIA

What stands out about the race Bobby Isaac won in April 1971 held at Greenville-Pickens Speedway in South Carolina?

Answers to the trivia questions are on pages 180–181.

laps. He wound up beating Cale Yarborough by 67.15 points for the championship.

"It was such a roller coaster of a day," Parsons said. "You went to the racetrack trying to win a championship. You crash on the 13th lap, and it's over. We didn't have any roll bars. It had ripped the roll cage out of the car, and we didn't have anything to fix it with. But there was an old car sitting there that didn't qualify for the race, and so we went down and cut the roll bars out of that car and put them in ours.

"It has always been such a strange thing. I don't remember being that emotional. We had been racing for the championship all year long. We had been in the lead since way back when, and we were supposed to win it.

"Winning a race is a lot more emotional, because they throw the checkered flag and it's over. But a season-long championship, it's just so stressful and it's every race. When it was over with, it was, 'Phew. Thank God that's over.'"

In the summer of 2006, Parsons was diagnosed with lung cancer, though he'd given up smoking 30 years earlier. He found out soon enough that the racing community hadn't changed all that much.

"It's just like in my sickness now. I don't know how many people have said, 'If there's anything I can do for you...If you want me to drive you somewhere, pick something up, just let me know,'" Parsons said. "It was the same thing on that Sunday. You know, racing is just a big family." —J.M.

Cale's Long, Hard Fight

There's not much three-time NASCAR champion Cale Yarborough hasn't tried, as long as it had an element of danger attached.

In his many lives, he was a skydiver before skydiving came into fashion, a thrill-car driver, a semipro football player, and a Golden Gloves boxer. He wrestled an alligator—by accident—and was bitten by a rattlesnake (the rattlesnake died). He once fell out of an airplane, and he landed one on a dirt road in the middle of a thunderstorm.

Somewhere in his many incarnations, he worked in "race-car driver."

"I raced during high school, and I was pretty hooked at an early age," Yarborough once said. "I knew that was what I wanted to do. Whether I could do it or not, I didn't know. I knew it would be a long, hard fight, but I knew that was what I wanted to do."

The key words here are "long," "hard," and "fight." If race-car driving didn't contain all three of those elements, Yarborough would probably have spent his life cutting pulpwood, farming, or raising turkeys—all three of which he also tried.

But if anyone were ever born to a profession, it might have been the rugged little man from Sardis, South Carolina. If you were to jot down a list of three of the hardest chargers who ever lived, that list would likely include Curtis Turner, Junior Johnson, and Yarborough. Not necessarily in that order.

Turner was a millionaire who raced for the hell of it, a guy who'd tear up your race car and his to get a win. Johnson was an ex-bootlegger for whom going around in circles was tame compared to being chased on squirrelly mountain roads with a car full of illegal booze.

Yarborough was, well, Yarborough.

He had one of the most successful careers of anyone in racing, ever. His 83 Winston Cup wins is fifth on the all-time wins list. He is the only man to ever win three consecutive Winston Cup championships (1976–78). He won the Daytona 500 four times, and his record five wins in the Southern 500 went unmatched for 20 years until Jeff Gordon tied it in 2002.

TRIVIA

Who holds the record for the most poles in one season?

Answers to the trivia questions are on pages 180–181.

Yarborough sneaked under the fence to see his first Southern 500 in 1951, and he slipped into his buddy Bobby Weatherly's race car in 1957 to drive it for the first time—before he reached legal age.

He drove for the worst, for himself, and for the best. Yarborough went nine seasons, racing only a few a year, until he got his first win at Valdosta, Georgia, in 1965.

He drove for Herman "Turtle" Beam, a man so cautious he once told Yarborough to slow down for fear he'd scratch up his car. Banjo Matthews gave him his first big break, but winning didn't become a regular feature of Yarborough's game until he joined the Wood Brothers in the late 1960s. Between 1966 and 1970, Yarborough won 13 races for the Woods. However, it wasn't until he hooked up with Johnson, the laconic mountain man from North Carolina, that Yarborough found his racing soul mate.

TRIVIA

Cale Yarborough did something twice in his career that no other Cup driver has been able to accomplish even once. What was it?

Answers to the trivia questions are on pages 180–181.

In his youth, Johnson was known as the "Wild Man from Wilkes County," and raced to live up to that nickname. As a team owner, the only part of the car he wanted back was the steering wheel, so long as his driver tore up the rest of the car in pursuit of a win.

Johnson and Yarborough made a formidable pair. As Johnson's driver between 1973 and 1980, Yarborough won 55 of his races and all three of his championships. And he lost as spectacularly as he won.

One of the sport's all-time legends, Cale Yarborough, receives a trophy after winning the 1970 Motor State 400 in Michigan.

When he and Donnie Allison crashed on the final lap of the 1979 Daytona 500, the fight between Yarborough and the Allison brothers (Bobby joined in) became part of racing lore. And since that was the first Daytona 500 shown on live TV, it was credited for giving NASCAR a huge boost as a spectator sport.

"I think it was a turning point in NASCAR, and that's why people remember it," Yarborough said. "You would think that people would forget about that eventually, but I'll tell you what: if I'm going to a function, I'll bet a hundred people will mention that story to me. They don't forget."

The most surprising thing about Yarborough's driving career is that he quit—or at least tapered off—at the top of his game.

He had won a half a dozen races with Johnson in 1980 when he realized there were more important things than racing. He was leaving for a sponsor affair when he noticed his three daughters moping about on the back porch. He told them to go bike riding or something, and they told him he hadn't fixed one of their bikes, like he'd promised weeks earlier.

Yarborough took off his tie, called the sponsor and canceled, and called Johnson and told him he was cutting back.

Victory Leaders in NASCAR's Premier Series (1970–79)

	Driver	Wins	Races	Top 5s	Poles	Earnings
1.	Richard Petty	89	326	221	41	$3,575,379
2.	Cale Yarborough	52	234	151	29	$3,053,931
3.	David Pearson	47	186	118	57	$1,801,427
4.	Bobby Allison	41	313	176	43	$2,385,051
5.	Darrell Waltrip	22	159	84	16	$1,778,971
6.	Bobby Isaac	16	137	64	26	$557,460
7.	Buddy Baker	14	228	107	22	$1,778,655
8.	Donnie Allison	8	154	55	13	$800,677
9.	Neil Bonnett	5	91	17	14	$471,426
10.	A.J. Foyt	5	45	18	8	$366,219

Source: www.racing-reference.info

"That story is true," Yarborough said. "It was hard to tell Junior, because I knew he and I could win a lot more championships together. But you have to weigh everything out and see what's more important. Junior understood."

Though Yarborough had 14 more wins after that, driving for M.C. Anderson and Harry Ranier, he never raced a full season after 1980. He tried his hand at team ownership again, driving for himself in 1987 and 1988, and got one victory as an owner when John Andretti won the Pepsi 400 at Daytona in 1997. As an owner, however, the game simply became too expensive to play. He sold his team after the 1998 season and retired to his 1,300-acre farm near Sardis.

"Nothing would suit me better than being a successful Winston Cup team owner," Yarborough said when he quit, "but that will never happen. The sponsorships are not there, the people aren't there. It would be a task."

When reminded that he never seemed like a man to shirk a task, Yarborough chuckled, "No, but I'm just doing other tasks now."

Now, instead of daughters, it's grandkids. But there's always a bike needing to be fixed.—J.M.

Keeping the Jaws Working

It was Darrell Waltrip himself who came up with the nickname "Ol' DW" late in his own driving career, long after he realized he should have hung up his helmet and gone on to that great television booth on high—where he has become a star all over again.

In his driving heyday, others had different names for Waltrip. They would sometimes call him "Daring Darrell" or "Dirty Darrell." But there was one more that really stuck. In the 1977 Southern 500, Waltrip and Cale Yarborough's memorable battle came to a crunching halt late in the race when both wanted the same spot in Darlington's infamous third turn. Neither backed off, and the result was a five-car wreck.

After the race, D.K. Ulrich, one of the innocent bystanders, approached Yarborough and asked why he took him out.

"I didn't touch you," Yarborough snarled. "Jaws hit you."

"Who?"

"Jaws. Jaws Waltrip hit you."

In his prime, that nickname fit him to a T. Waltrip would eat your car alive with his skill and boldness on the racetrack, and then have the audacity to not only tell everybody how he did it, but also tell them why. The brash kid from Owensboro, Kentucky, didn't win all the battles on the racetrack, but nobody beat him in the war of words.

Most of the drivers didn't like the trash-talking, but track promoters—and some fans—ate it up. The more controversial Waltrip was and the more outlandish things he said, the better. They laughed all the way to the bank. And so did Waltrip.

Waltrip moved to Nashville (Franklin, Tennessee, actually), which was a hotbed of racing, early in his driving career, and didn't

SEASON TO REMEMBER

Darrell Waltrip—1981–82

There was never a time when Darrell Waltrip didn't talk the talk. But after bolting from his ride with the DiGard team after the 1980 season to join car owner Junior Johnson's operation, over the next two seasons he absolutely walked the walk, too. Waltrip won 12 races in 1981 and came back the next year and did the same thing all over again. In addition to those 24 victories, Waltrip finished in the top 10 in 45 of 61 races on his way to back-to-back titles.

try his hand at NASCAR's elite circuit until 1972, when he managed to run five races out of his own pocket. Those were the days before multimillion-dollar contracts for unknown kids, but he didn't stay in that category for long.

Waltrip won his first race at Nashville early in 1975, driving his own car, then latched on with Bill Gardner's well-funded DiGard Racing team later in the season and won again at Richmond.

Typical of Waltrip, after his first win he said, "I figured I'd have won a race a lot sooner than this."

He won quite a few after. Before his acrimonious breakup with Gardner in 1980, Waltrip had put 27 victories in his dossier and was hungry for more. It may have been a matter of fortuitous timing, or maybe Waltrip put himself in the right place at the right time, but just as Waltrip was ready to say good-bye to DiGard, Yarborough got fed up with the exhausting lifestyle of full-time racing and told legendary car owner Junior Johnson he wanted out. Yarborough and Johnson had won championships in 1976, 1977, and 1978, but Johnson acceded to his three-time champion's wishes. Johnson wasn't all that infatuated with "that mouthy Waltrip boy," either—but Johnson also knew a driver when he saw one, and he hired him on the spot.

The pair won 12 races and the championship in each of the next two seasons, and six and seven races in 1983 and 1984, respectively. Despite winning "only" three races in 1985, Waltrip took his third and last title.

That was the year Bill Elliott won 11 of 28 races, including three of the four Winston Million events. But Elliott lost his stride late in the season when Waltrip began tossing barbs at the slow-talking Elliott clan.

"It ain't no fun needling the Elliott boys," Waltrip said. "They won't talk back at you. They just stand and look at you."

He won three races more in 1986 but lost the championship to Dale Earnhardt.

Darrell Waltrip, known for his trash-talking as much as for his aggressive style on the track, hoists the trophy from the 1982 Talladega 500.

Darrell's Darts

Darrell Waltrip had one of the quickest—and sharpest—tongues in racing. A few of his jabs:

"I was just going to show them where the blue-light specials were." Explaining why, after fans booed lustily when he won, Waltrip, over the PA system, invited them to meet him in the parking lot at the local K-Mart, which was his sponsor at the time.

"They were saying, 'Dewww! Dewww!'"
Same scene, when Mountain Dew was paying the bills.

"You picked a fine time to leave me, loose wheel."
After David Pearson's breakup with the Wood Brothers team, a week after Pearson ran out of the pits at Darlington in 1979—in an attempt to keep Waltrip from lapping him—with no lug nuts on the left side of his car.

In June of that year, Waltrip announced he was leaving Johnson to go with a relative newcomer, Rick Hendrick. As a parting shot, he told the press he was "getting off an old mule and onto a thoroughbred."

Johnson's answer was succinct: "I've had a jackass driving my car, and now I'm rid of him."

Some say that the best and worst day of Waltrip's life was September 17, 1987. After 17 years of marriage, Waltrip's wife, Stevie, gave birth to their first child, Jessica Leigh. Maybe Waltrip, who had spent a career believing he was bulletproof, suddenly realized his mortality. Maybe not. But whatever the reason, he became less daring, and it showed.

Johnson's opinion was that it could be traced back to a savage crash in the 1983 Daytona 500, when Waltrip was knocked unconscious. He didn't even remember racing the next week at Richmond, Johnson said.

"Darrell was hurt more than any of us suspected," Johnson said. "It didn't show for a long time...[but] it had a far-reaching effect."

Waltrip won his share of races, nine, with Hendrick between 1987 and 1990, and even won five in the first two years after he got caught up in the driver/owner craze of the early 1990s, but his days as "Jaws" were pretty much over.

On the weekend of the 2000 NAPA 500 in Atlanta, Waltrip's last race, the man who had scored 84 career Winston Cup victories, tied for third on the all-time list, and won three titles, Waltrip admitted what everyone else had known. "I wish I'd have quit a little sooner," Waltrip said. "These last seven or eight years have been brutal, but there have been some high points. It's not a bed of roses. It's not always as easy as it looks and things don't turn out the way you thought they were going to, but I've survived."

Not only survived, but flourished.

When Waltrip did walk away from the sport, he didn't have to walk far. He retired and moved immediately into the broadcasting booth as Fox Sports kicked off NASCAR's first comprehensive television contract with the start of the 2001 season. Joining veteran announcer Mike Joy and former crew chief Larry McReynolds in the booth for Fox, Waltrip regularly shows flashes of the kind of wit that nourished him through a stellar career.—J.M.

EARN-HARDT!

A statue that honors seven-time NASCAR Cup champion Dale Earnhardt in his hometown of Kannapolis, North Carolina, stands nine feet tall.

That seems about right.

There is a Paul Bunyan quality to the story of this great champion's life and career, and his figure still looms large over the sport he helped transform even after his tragic death.

Much has been written and said about how Earnhardt's death in a crash on the final lap of the 2001 Daytona 500 became the catalyst for major changes in NASCAR. Safety initiatives that were inching along at an evolutionary pace turned into a revolution with a markedly accelerated pace of development bringing innovation and improvements to the cars and the tracks used in stock-car racing virtually overnight.

But Earnhardt in many ways was always an agent for change and growth in a sport he was born into. The son of legendary short-track racer Ralph Earnhardt, Dale Earnhardt became a living bridge from the days when NASCAR thrived on those bullrings to the era of the modern stadium-style superspeedways

H.A. "Humpy" Wheeler, president of Lowe's Motor Speedway, calls Earnhardt the "last of the red-dirt racers." That's the right place to start when remembering Earnhardt, because it was those small dirt tracks of the Carolinas where he went to see Ralph drive that Dale found that need for speed.

By age 16, Dale had decided to quit school and try to chase his racing dreams. Ralph, who'd kept his job at the textile mill in

Dale Earnhardt helped take the sport from the bullrings to today's superspeedways, and he continues to be a catalyst for change years after his death.

Kannapolis for most of the time he was racing, didn't like his son's decision. But there was really no way anybody was ever going to keep Dale Earnhardt off a racetrack.

The early years were tough ones.

In those days, there were no "driver development" programs in which teenagers with talent were snapped up quickly by big-time teams and given high-profile rides before they were old enough to rent a car to drive on the street. Like anyone else with dreams of making it to NASCAR, Dale Earnhardt had to start on the short tracks and learn by the seat of his pants.

One night, at the Metrolina Fairgrounds near Charlotte, the lesson came directly from his dad. Dale was running in one of the smaller series at the track, but a less-than-full field allowed him to be in the same event as Ralph. Late in the race Dale was running fourth, but he was so far behind that the leader lapped him. That leader was, of

SEASON TO REMEMBER
Dale Earnhardt—1987

Dale Earnhardt had to wait until 1998 before he finally won the Daytona 500, but that was about the only race he didn't win at the start of his 1987 season. Earnhardt finished fifth at Daytona, but then won Rockingham and Richmond. After a 16th-place finish at Atlanta, Earnhardt won Darlington, North Wilkesboro, Bristol, and Martinsville. With six wins in eight races, he was well on his way to a third career championship and a second straight at Richard Childress Racing. Earnhardt later won the Southern 500 at Darlington in between wins at Bristol and Richmond, and finished the year with a career-best 11 victories.

course, Ralph, who pulled in behind his son and literally pushed him to a third-place finish—which put Dale in the money that night.

Dale got married at 17, became a father for the first time at 18 when Kerry was born, and got a divorce at age 19. Raising a family at that age would have been tough enough without racing taking money out of the equation. Earnhardt kept racing every time he could, working as a mechanic and in other jobs to keep his dream alive.

He got married again, to Brenda Gee, in 1971 and they had two children, Kelley and Dale Jr. In 1973, Ralph Earnhardt died of a heart attack while working in the garage at his home in Kannapolis.

Earnhardt ran his first Winston Cup race at Charlotte Motor Speedway in May 1975, finishing 22nd in a car owned by Ed Negre. In all, though, it took him more than a decade to finally get a legitimate shot at racing among NASCAR's best. Once he finally got that shot, Earnhardt wasn't about to let go.

In 1979, car owner Rod Osterlund put Earnhardt in his No. 2 cars. He got his first victory on April 1 at Bristol Motor Speedway, leading 163 laps in the Southeastern 500 to beat Bobby Allison, Darrell Waltrip, and Richard Petty. Despite missing four races with a broken collarbone, Earnhardt had 11 top-five finishes and 17 top-10s on his way to winning Rookie of the Year honors.

The next season, Earnhardt won five more races and, amazingly to many, the Winston Cup title. Suddenly, instead of having to borrow money for tires on Friday so he could race on Saturday night and hope to win enough to pay the money back on Monday, Earnhardt was near the $1 million mark in career earnings and was the talk of the sport.

In 1981, however, Osterlund sold his team in the middle of the season to J.D. Stacy, and Earnhardt left shortly thereafter. He spent the final races of that year driving for Richard Childress, who'd been driving the cars he owned and knew that he didn't yet have the kind of team Earnhardt should be with.

Earnhardt spent the next two seasons driving Fords owned by NASCAR legend Bud Moore while Ricky Rudd helped Childress build his team. But in 1984, Rudd and Earnhardt basically swapped seats, and Earnhardt and Childress were united for what would become one of the sport's great all-time pairings.

From 1984 through the end of the 2000 season, Earnhardt would win 67 races in Chevrolets owned by Childress. They won their first championship together in 1986, added another one in 1987, and wound up winning a total of six in nine seasons that allowed Earnhardt to match Richard Petty among drivers with seven career titles and drew Childress even with Junior Johnson with six championships as an owner.

Earnhardt and Childress not only won races and championships together; they also helped to change the economic formula for success in NASCAR. With the backing he got in sponsorships, first with Wrangler blue jeans and then with General Motors itself, Earnhardt became one of the first drivers to successfully mine revenue from the merchandising and endorsement streams beginning to flow through the growing sport.

Earnhardt's image, characterized by the "One Tough Customer" slogan used by Wrangler in its marketing campaigns, was a hit with millions of fans. That persona carried over to the racetrack, and when GM Goodwrench took over as sponsor and Earnhardt's car became an all-black No. 3 Chevrolet, he morphed into the "Intimidator."

TRIVIA

Only six drivers have led more than 20,000 laps in their Cup careers. Name them.

Answers to the trivia questions are on pages 180–181.

It was said that many drivers who got moved out of the way by Ralph Earnhardt eventually started moving over when they saw him coming, and that's exactly what started happening with Dale, too. Because he won so often and because he sometimes imposed his will—or his bumper—on his opponents, Earnhardt became the kind of driver about whom nobody was neutral. His fans came to the track hoping to see the No. 3 car beat everyone else, while most other drivers' fans came hoping and praying that Earnhardt would wreck and finish last.

Over the course of his brilliant career, Earnhardt was part of some of the sport's most memorable events. His victory in the 1985 running of the all-star race at Charlotte featured the so-called pass in the grass, and he won one or more races in each of 15 consecutive seasons beginning in 1982.

He was involved in several major crashes, including a wreck at Talladega in 1996 in which he suffered a broken collarbone and sternum that forced him to get out of his car the following race at Indianapolis. One week later, though, Earnhardt drove despite the injuries and won the pole for a road-course race at Watkins Glen.

Earnhardt was particularly masterful in restrictor-plate races at Daytona and Talladega. Even though he often said publicly that he hated the plates that restrict air flowing into a car's carburetor and therefore choke off horsepower to slow the cars down, Earnhardt's 11 career plate victories still lead all drivers.

Earnhardt would have had even more plate-race victories had it not been for a career filled with horrible luck in the sport's biggest race, the Daytona 500. Several times in his career Earnhardt seem-ingly had that race won, only to have something bizarre happen. In 1990, for instance, Earnhardt was leading on the final lap when he ran over a piece of debris that fell off another car and cut a tire, allowing Derrike Cope to score an unlikely victory.

By 1998, Earnhardt had been in 19 Daytona 500s without a victory. Finally, however, on February 15 of that year, he led 107 laps and held off Bobby Labonte as they raced back to a yellow flag that effectively ended the race. Earnhardt had finally won the 500. As he came down pit road to go to victory lane, members of virtually every crew in the sport lined up to offer their congratulations.

Earnhardt pulled off into the infield grass and celebrated his victory with a series of "doughnuts." When he was done, it appeared as though he'd cut a large "3" in the grass—something he'd always swear he did on purpose while grinning in a way that almost made you believe him. As the sun set on Daytona that day, fans were in the grass digging up chunks of sod to take home as souvenirs.

At Bristol in August 1999, Earnhardt was involved in a last-lap incident with Terry Labonte and went on to score yet another controversial victory. "I didn't mean to wreck him," Earnhardt said that night. "I just wanted to rattle his cage."

A little more than a year later, Earnhardt was trapped at the back of the pack after a late-race caution at Talladega. With five laps left, he was running 18th and seemingly had no shot to rack up yet another plate-race victory. But anyone who believed Earnhardt was out of it underestimated his talent and determination. By the time he took the white flag, Earnhardt was in the lead and on the way to his 76th career victory.

That afternoon, as Earnhardt came to the press box for his post-race interview, fans thronged in his path as though they were welcoming home a conquering hero. And in many ways, they were. By that point in his career, Earnhardt's official winnings were at more than $40 million, but the blue-collar fans at the core of NASCAR's base still somehow never felt Earnhardt had lost touch with them.

That, perhaps better than anything else, explains why Earnhardt's death in the Daytona 500 the next year touched race fans so deeply.

In spite of all he had done, in spite of all the victories and championships and the fame and fortune that had come with them, in spite of the fact that he had become—like the statue they would eventually build in his hometown in his honor—larger than life, he was still exactly who he'd always been.

He was Earnhardt.—D.P.

Boys Will Be Boys

There's rarely a dull moment when you're dealing with Bruton Smith and H.A. "Humpy" Wheeler. And perhaps that's because they're both still little boys at heart.

Smith, the owner of Lowe's Motor Speedway in Charlotte, North Carolina, and several other NASCAR tracks in the Speedway Motorsports Inc. family, remembers being about eight years old when he went to the fair near his home in the little town of Oakboro, North Carolina, and saw Lucky Teeter's daredevil act.

"He jumped over a bus in a car," Smith said. "Man, that was awesome to see that car hanging in the air, and then when it landed the wheel covers popped off and, I think, one tire blew out. That was a spectacle."

Wheeler, the president of Lowe's Motor Speedway and the man widely regarded as the premiere promotional genius working in automobile racing today, always tries to remember what it was like when he was a 12-year-old boy going to sporting events. The sense that something big was about to happen kept him coming back.

It's almost as though Wheeler and Smith were destined to work together, and they've done that off and on for nearly 50 years.

Their similarities run deep.

Both grew up in North Carolina—Smith on a farm in Oakboro and Wheeler in the town of Belmont, where his father, Howard, was the athletics director at a small Catholic college. It was the elder Wheeler, in fact, who was first called "Humpy" because he liked to smoke Camel cigarettes when he was a young man. The nickname stuck and was passed down a generation.

Bruton Smith (right) and H.A. "Humpy" Wheeler have been working together on and off for nearly 50 years.

Both Smith and Wheeler were athletes in school. Smith was named "most athletic"—as well as "most popular" and "most conceited"—in his high school yearbook. Wheeler played football and boxed in Golden Gloves while at the University of South Carolina.

They both also tried their hands at driving race cars. Smith's mother, Mollie, begged her son to quit racing when he was a teenager and finally resorted to praying about that desire. "When she started to pray," Smith said, "I felt she was fighting dirty and I'd better stop. It wasn't just going against Mom. It was going against God."

Smith and Wheeler both eventually found their way into the business side of racing, promoting events at various dirt tracks across the Carolinas and the Southeast. When NASCAR began in 1949, in fact, the 23-year-old Smith was still running a rival series to Bill France's called the National Stock Car Racing Association. When Smith was drafted into the military two years later, however, the

TOP 10

Most Unusual Tracks Used for NASCAR Races

1. Augusta International Speedway: A three-mile road course in Augusta, Georgia (as compared to Watkins Glen's 2.45 miles), Augusta had 21 turns (there are 11 at the Glen). Fireball Roberts won the only Grand National event held there, on November 17, 1963.
2. Soldier Field: That's right, the home of "Da Bears." A half-mile paved track around the gridiron. Roberts won the only Grand National event held there, on July 21, 1956.
3. Langhorne Speedway: A one-mile dirt track in Langhorne, Pennsylvania, laid out in a near-perfect circle. NASCAR raced there from 1949 to 1957 and, next to Darlington, it was considered the toughest track because there were no straightaways on which to catch your breath.
4. Ontario Motor Speedway: Built in 1970 in Ontario, California, the 2.5-mile rectangular track was patterned after Indianapolis Motor Speedway. It sported elevators, restaurants, and suites long before that became the norm.
5. Oakland Stadium: Bristol Motor Speedway is a flat track by comparison. At the Oakland, California, track, drivers had to negotiate 45-degree banking at one end and an incredible 60 degrees at the other. When NASCAR went there in 1954, track officials tried to take some of the steepness out of the banking by piling dirt in the turns. That made it one of the only tracks in history to have paved straightaways and dirt turns.
6. Lakewood Speedway: Lakewood Speedway in Atlanta was a scary one-mile dirt track that had the little-end, big-end feel of Darlington. But the scariest part was that a lake took up most of the infield. No one drowned, but a lot went swimming.
7. North Wilkesboro Speedway: The "home track" of superstar Junior Johnson, the little .625-mile oval in North Carolina had a backstretch that went uphill and a front stretch that went downhill.

8. Memphis-Arkansas Speedway: Another scary track. A mile and a half around, the LeHi, Arkansas, facility hosted five Grand National races in the 1950s. The largest dirt track ever used by NASCAR, it had only a wooden guard rail, which Lee Petty once went through, landing in a lake.

9. Martinsville Speedway: One of the few survivors to the modern era, the little half-mile track in Martinsville, Virginia, was a scary place for fans. If you didn't have a reserved seat, you stood on a dirt embankment some five feet high, right in the turns.

10. Daytona Beach and Road Course: A 4.1-mile course that consisted of half pavement, half seashore, it preceded Daytona International Speedway as the place to be in Daytona. Racers sped north along the strand, cut left on a bumpy ride through the sand dunes, then raced back down Highway A1A to the unpaved south turn before doing it all over. Races were scheduled according to the tidal charts.

NSCRA died out and NASCAR's ascension to prominence in the stock-car racing world was beginning.

Wheeler, meanwhile, cut his teeth at a dirt track called Robinwood Speedway in Gastonia, North Carolina. To this day, Wheeler still cites lessons he learned in running that track. In fact, there's a dirt bullring across the street from Lowe's Motor Speedway right now, and when races are held there Wheeler insists that everything possible be done to keep the dust down so fans don't go home covered with a fine red film.

Wheeler's and Smith's paths merged after financial realities forced a shotgun wedding between Smith and the legendary driver Curtis Turner. Both Turner and Smith wanted to build a racetrack near Charlotte, but they had to face the fact that they'd be lucky to pull it off working together much less doing it individually. The track was plagued by construction delays and the first race, the World 600 in 1960, was delayed by a month until the track could be finished.

Even then, chunks of asphalt came up out of the track during the event to the point that the first 600-mile race in NASCAR history became a war of attrition. Drivers and crew chiefs attached thick wire screens to their radiators to keep projectiles from rupturing them, but car after car fell out because of the conditions until Joe Lee Johnson got the victory.

Wheeler was working with Smith at the time. His main memory of the ordeal is that when the race finally reached its halfway point— meaning it would be an official race and not have to be resumed the next day if bad weather intervened—Wheeler laid down in the control tower to take a nap. It was the first sleep he'd had in days.

The financial hurdles Smith and Turner had tried to clear in getting Charlotte Motor Speedway built proved too difficult to overcome. The track fell into debt and eventually, bankruptcy. Smith was forced out and wound up in the auto-dealership business, first as a salesman and eventually as the owner of his first dealership in Rockford, Illinois.

Wheeler, meanwhile, spent seven years working with Firestone, first as a publicist and later as its director of motorsports, and says that helped him learn what should and shouldn't be done in the business.

Smith, meanwhile, was rebuilding his fortune in the car business. By the mid-1970s he was back in Charlotte and had bought up enough stock to regain control of Charlotte Motor Speedway. Smith hired Wheeler as "director of development" in 1975, and a few months later when Richard Howard, who'd been the track's general manager since Smith's ouster, resigned Wheeler was promoted to that post.

Wheeler's first World 600 was in 1976, and it provided more valuable lessons. That year, Janet Guthrie was trying to make history by qualifying for the Indianapolis 500. Wheeler decided to contact her and offer her a car for the NASCAR race in Charlotte on the same day, should she fail to get into the race in Indianapolis. That's what happened, and Guthrie wound up racing in Charlotte.

"That's the first time we ever sold out the 600," Wheeler said. "We were selling single tickets, which you never sell all of. Taxicabs

"Man versus Shark: One Must Die"

As part of race week activities at Charlotte Motor Speedway, Humpy Wheeler took to employing an endurance swimmer named Moon Huffstetler to try to break the world record for treading water.

After a couple of times, though, Wheeler thought the stunt was getting a little stale. About this time the movie *Jaws* was all the rage, so one member of Wheeler's staff joked about putting a shark in the tank with Huffstetler.

Everyone laughed—except Wheeler. "That might work!" he said. The staff went into a panic, figuring that surely the shark would devour the swimmer. Wheeler opined that Huffstetler might be fitted with a special suit to protect him, but the staff pointed out that swimming for hours at a time in such a suit might be taxing.

The idea was dropped, but at one point someone in the room mentioned that such a stunt, if tried, would surely bring animal rights protesters to the scene.

"If it doesn't," Wheeler said, "you'd better hire some."

were pulling up in front of the speedway and women were getting out, coming to see Janet Guthrie race."

One of the things Wheeler took from that day was that his racetrack didn't have enough bathrooms for female race fans. Today, one of the cornerstones of Wheeler's philosophy for running a track is to remember "the three *T*s—traffic, toilets, and trash."

One of the many reasons Smith and Wheeler have worked so well together over the years is that neither is afraid of big ideas. Since Smith regained control in 1975, Charlotte Motor Speedway has become the template for the modern stock-car facility.

It has expanded from around 65,000 seats to nearly 170,000. Luxury boxes line the massive grandstands along the front stretch of the 1.5-mile trioval. The Speedway Club, a high-end restaurant that is open year-round, sits atop the start/finish line. In 1983, everyone from television comedians to Wheeler himself thought Smith was crazy for building condominiums in Turn 1 of the track. Those condos are now worth many times their original price, and they've popped up at various other tracks around the country.

Smith took his company public, again against conventional wisdom, but since doing so Speedway Motorsports Inc. (SMI) has

Oooh, Oooh—That Smell

When Humpy Wheeler was promoting races at Robinwood Speedway in Gastonia, North Carolina, near his hometown of Belmont, he was also in charge of preparing the track on race day. This meant driving a truck filled with water used to create the tacky surface the cars needed to race on and to keep dust down so spectators could see the cars and wouldn't go home covered from head to toe. On one Saturday, however, Wheeler's water truck broke down. He could not get it to run. In a panic, he remembered he knew a man who pumped septic tanks for a living. He called and arranged to borrow the man's truck, then pumped out the tanker and filled it with what Wheeler thought was clean water.

As it turned out, the normal function of the septic tank truck had an impact on the water Wheeler used to wet down his track. After working all afternoon, he ran home to change clothes and came back to the race that night. When he arrived, he smelled a distinct odor that he knew wasn't about to go away.

"We're sorry about that smell tonight, folks," Wheeler had his announcer tell the crowd. "When the wind blows this way, sometimes we get that from the pulp mill."

Funny, but nobody ever smelled the pulp mill before that night—or after it, as long as Wheeler's water truck worked.

increased Smith's racing empire. Atlanta Motor Speedway and Bristol Motor Speedway were both transformed into massive facilities after SMI bought them. Smith then built Texas Motor Speedway near Fort Worth and opened it in 1997.

After years of wrangling with the France family, it now has two races each year, as do Atlanta, Bristol, and Lowe's Motor Speedway— the name of the Charlotte track after Smith sold naming rights. Infineon Raceway, a road course in Sonoma, California, has one race a year, as does, for now at least, Las Vegas Motor Speedway, which is the most recent track purchased by SMI. As has been the case at every track he owns, Smith has spent millions of dollars to upgrade the facilities at Sonoma and is just completing a massive project at Las Vegas in which the track has been reshaped and garage and media facilities in the infield have been completely reworked.

Smith will turn 80 in 2007, but he won't even entertain the notion of retirement.

"I don't even like that word," he said. "Retiring sounds like the end of the road. We have a lot of things to do yet. If I can keep this thing going for another 20 years maybe we'll get some stuff done. I have to accomplish more in the next 20 years than I have done in the past 20."

Ask Smith what he likes most about his job and he has a simple answer.

"You look at all of that mass of people," he said. "And you say, 'My goodness, all of these people are here to see something you're putting on.' That's a cool feeling."

That is, of course, another thing he shares with Wheeler.

Ed Clark, now president of Atlanta Motor Speedway, is one of several prominent figures in the sport today who trained under Wheeler at Charlotte.

"We had a race coming up, and at home I had come up with this brainstorm," Clark said. "I couldn't wait to bust in and tell Humpy about it. I had it all worked out and thought it all through, and I went in there and pitched the whole idea.

"Humpy said, 'Ed, that's good.' Then he said, 'What if we do this with it, and what if we did this, too.' And just like that, he'd taken a pretty good idea and made it great."

Jerry Gappens, the vice president for promotions and public relations at the Charlotte track, said Wheeler is a combination of Don King, Walt Disney, and P.T. Barnum.

"He's got the ability to promote like Don King, to take an event and make it seem like it's the biggest thing in the world," Gappens said. "He also has always had a vision of what the future is going to look like the way a Walt Disney or people like him did. And certainly, he's known for being a showman like P.T. Barnum, somebody who has always understood the importance of always having something going on all of the time."

Wheeler's legendary prerace shows have featured things like mock military invasions and a daredevil jumping over cars in a school bus—a reverse on the Lucky Teeter stunt that got the eight-year-old Bruton Smith's attention in the first place.

Once, Wheeler was standing in the Charlotte press box and overheard two motorsports journalists talking about the extravaganza unfolding before them.

"Next year," one of them said, "why don't they just put on a circus?"

The next year's prerace show? A circus, complete with an elephant on the pit road.

Like we said, when it comes to Bruton Smith and Humpy Wheeler, no idea is too big.—D.P.

Thrills, Spills, and Dollar Bills—All-Star Style

"Checkers or wreckers." Deep in their hearts, that's the motto every promoter who's ever staged an automobile race would like drivers to have—win or hit something trying.

But as the quest for championships became more and more the focus in NASCAR's top series, that primal urge in some competitors became a little bit suppressed. It changed, too, when the money got good enough where drivers reaching the sport's top level didn't have to win to pay their tire bills. Sponsors were writing some pretty nice checks, and the sport's top stars even started getting a base salary to go with the 40 percent or 50 percent of the team's earnings that had traditionally been their weekly stipend.

In 1985, with NASCAR looking to do anything it could to get national media attention turned its way, the folks at R.J. Reynolds Tobacco came up with an idea for an annual all-star race.

In its original form, only drivers who'd won races the previous season were eligible to run in the event. It would be a short race, like a sprint at a Saturday night short track. And it would pay $200,000 to the winner.

Understand that until that race the most any driver had ever won in one NASCAR event was $185,500, won by Bill Elliott in that year's Daytona 500. Many race winners that season earned less than $40,000 for their day's work, so $200,000 was more than enough to get their attention.

The first race was scheduled for 70 laps at the 1.5-mile Charlotte Motor Speedway, the day before the track's annual Coca-Cola 600.

The NASCAR all-star race nearly ended after only seven years? In 1991, R.J. Reynolds was considering whether to keep sponsoring the event after a five-year deal with Charlotte Motor Speedway ran out. During negotiations, track president H.A. "Humpy" Wheeler told RJR sports marketing chief T. Wayne Robertson that for the 1992 event, his track planned to add lights and run the race on Saturday night. Robertson loved the idea and moved forward. There was only one problem. "We didn't know whether we could do it or not," Wheeler said. Night races had been run at short tracks throughout NASCAR's history, but illuminating a 1.5-mile superspeedway had never been tried before. But in May 1992, the lights came on and a new era of NASCAR night racing began.

Darrell Waltrip knew his car owner, Junior Johnson, was serious about trying to win the event because he saw Johnson in the shop working on the engine himself.

"He said he was building me a set of 'sweet-potato rods,'" Waltrip said. "He called them that because they were fast and they were slick."

Twelve drivers started the race, and when the checkered flag flew, it was indeed Waltrip taking the victory. Just as he crossed the finish line, however, his engine erupted in smoke.

"I was working in the booth that day with Neil Bonnett, who was Darrell's teammate," said Mike Joy, who now is the anchor for Fox Sports's NASCAR broadcasts. "Neil started yelling, 'He clutched it! He clutched it!'" The implication was that Waltrip's engine problem was not coincidental, that the driver knew that he shouldn't let NASCAR officials get a look at the engine, at least not in its completely functional form, in the postrace inspection.

It was exactly the kind of start that RJR and the Charlotte track's officials were looking for to give the event an "outlaw" feel. Called the Winston in those days, the event has had several changes in name—it's now called the NASCAR Nextel All-Star Challenge—and in format. What hasn't changed over the years is that NASCAR's all-star race has had a propensity to produce some of the sport's more memorable moments.

That, however, does not necessarily include the second event. It was scheduled for Mother's Day in 1986 at Atlanta Motor Speedway, and the announced crowd was 18,500. Those who were actually there say there might not have been half that many actually in attendance. Only 10 cars were in the field, and Georgia native Bill Elliott completely dominated the race.

That's the only time in the event's history it has not been held at the Charlotte track. When it came back in 1987, the Winston provided one of the great battles in NASCAR lore, featuring what's come to be known as Dale Earnhardt's pass in the grass.

As is the case with most legends, there are some factual issues about what happened that day. The race had been moved to one week before the Coca-Cola 600 and had been given a new format dividing it into three segments of 75 laps, 50 laps, and then 10 laps.

Geoff Bodine and Bill Elliott, by virtue of their finish in the second segment, started the final segment on the front row.

Tony Stewart (20) rams Matt Kenseth into the wall during the 2006 Nextel All-Star Challenge at Charlotte Motor Speedway.

TOP 5

Most Memorable Moments in NASCAR's All-Star Race

1. **1987**—The pass in the grass: Dale Earnhardt holds the lead despite being run down through the infield grass while battling Bill Elliott in the final segment. Elliott and Geoff Bodine, who also got wrecked in the final segment, go home mad. Earnhardt goes to victory lane.

2. **1992**—"One Hot Night": Charlotte Motor Speedway uses "One Hot Night" as the marketing slogan for the first all-star event under the lights, and the race lives up to that. On the final lap, Kyle Petty and Dale Earnhardt are battling for the lead when they touch. Earnhardt spins in Turn 4, and Petty bobbles trying not to wreck, too. Davey Allison, who'd been running third, pounces on the opportunity and edges Petty at the finish line to win. Allison spins just after taking the checkered flag, crashing into the Turn 1 wall. He suffered a concussion and went to the hospital instead of victory lane.

3. **1989**—Rusty versus D.W.: Coming to the white flag in the final segment, Rusty Wallace taps the rear of Darrell Waltrip's car and sends Waltrip through the trioval grass. Waltrip contends he should be second on the restart, since caution laps don't count, but NASCAR says no. Wallace goes on to win. "I hope he chokes on that $200,000," Waltrip said of Wallace's winner's share of the purse.

4. **2001**—Do over!: The all-star race begins under threatening skies, and as the field runs into Turn 1 the rain begins. With treadless tires on their cars, several drivers wreck on the slick track. Since it's not a points race, however, NASCAR allows teams involved to get out their backup cars and get them ready for the start once

the rain abates. Jeff Gordon's team is one of these, and he leads all 10 laps of the final segment for his third career all-star victory.

5. **1985**—D.W. blows it: Darrell Waltrip wins the inaugural race, blowing his engine just as he takes the checkered flag. Did he do it on purpose so NASCAR in postrace inspection couldn't get a good look at the engine car owner Junior Johnson built for him?

Earnhardt and Tim Richmond, in his first racing action of the 1987 season after a bout with AIDS-related pneumonia, were on Row 2.

At the green flag, Bodine jumped into the lead. Earnhardt came to the outside of Elliott's car and crowded Elliott down toward the apron. Elliott wobbled and spun, clipping Bodine's bumper and spinning him, too.

Earnhardt took the lead. Caution-flag laps didn't count in the all-star race, but Earnhardt had the lead. Elliott and Earnhardt kept battling and, with seven laps left, they rubbed fenders coming off Turn 4.

Elliott pinched Earnhardt toward the inside of the track as they came toward the dogleg front stretch on the Charlotte track. Earnhardt's left wheels ran off into the grass in the trioval, but he never took his foot off the accelerator. It wasn't technically a "pass in the grass," you see, because Earnhardt had the lead when he went into the grass and he also had it when he came out.

Two laps later, Earnhardt moved Elliott up the track toward the Turn 4 wall in retaliation. Elliott blew a tire and fell a lap behind, but after Earnhardt beat Terry Labonte and Richmond to the finish line, Elliott waited on Earnhardt to come around on his cool-down lap and went after Earnhardt's Chevrolet with his Ford.

Bodine mistakenly thought it had been Earnhardt who'd wrecked him, too. So he also gave Earnhardt a postrace tap.

"If a man has to run over you to beat you, it's time for this stuff to stop," Elliott said. "He pulled over to let me pass, then ran me into the wall. I'd say that was done deliberately."

Earnhardt was fined, and Elliott and Bodine were reprimanded. But Charlotte Motor Speedway promoter Humpy Wheeler and T. Wayne Robertson, who was head of RJR's marketing arm, couldn't have been happier. And so began the rich and colorful history of what has evolved into one of the most anticipated events on the annual NASCAR calendar.

In subsequent seasons, the stakes got higher. In 2000, first prize increased to $500,000. In 2002, it became $750,000, and the following year it went to $1 million. Earnhardt and Jeff Gordon lead all drivers with three career all-star victories, with Davey Allison, Mark Martin, Terry Labonte, and Jimmie Johnson, the 2006 champion, each having two victories.—D.P.

Million Dollar Bill

Bill Elliott was born 20 years too late.

If he'd have begun his NASCAR racing career in 1956 instead of 1976, he'd have fit right in. For starters, Elliott loved working on his car as much as he did driving it. Second, if he'd come along earlier he probably would have spent his entire career racing with his brothers Dan and Ernie, not making much money, but loving every minute of it.

He probably also would have become "Awesome Bill from Dawsonville," because he was that good. But this much is certain: he'd never have become known as "Million Dollar Bill."

In 2004 Elliott went into a genteel semiretirement, racing here and there for several teams in the Nextel Cup Series. He didn't—and doesn't—need the money. At the end of the 2003 season, he had earned over $30 million in career winnings and maybe twice that much in endorsement fees and souvenir sales.

But in 1976, when he, his brothers, and a rag-tag bunch from Dahlonega, Georgia, hauled a 1973 Ford Torino over to Rockingham, North Carolina, to try their hand at the big-time, a million dollars was a long way off.

"I'll never forget it," Elliott said. "They had just so many garage stalls, and we were out there in the sand working on our car. 'Rookies' wouldn't describe us. The night before the race, we had a bunch of guys come up to help us on race day, and I'll bet we slept 13 or 14 in the motel room. There were bodies laying everywhere.

"We worked hard and didn't know any better."

They didn't get much out of that opening foray, either. Elliott qualified 34th and finished 33rd, running only 32 laps before his oil pump burned slap up. He won $640.

DID YOU KNOW...

The Ford Thunderbird in which Bill Elliott won the Winston Million bonus in 1985 sits in the National Motorsports Press Association's Hall of Fame at Darlington Raceway, but it's not the No. 9 he made famous?

Somewhere in the preparation of the car for that particular race, somebody goofed. The roof decal was put on backward. Instead of a "9" on its roof, the car has either a "6" or a lower case "e," depending on which side you're standing on.

"They took six cars the last day [of qualifying] and we were third quickest the last day," Elliott said. "We were so happy to make the race that we forgot to unblock the oil cooler before the race started. We went there with one goal: to make the race. Lord, I was lucky to be there, and that's the way I looked at it."

After the team hooked up with Harry Melling as a sponsor in 1982, Elliott made a steady progression, getting his first Winston Cup win in 1983 and three more in 1984. But in 1985 he exploded onto the racing scene, catching the biggest payday in NASCAR history to that point and catapulting himself into the kind of limelight he'd never be comfortable with.

Winston Cup Series sponsor R.J. Reynolds came up with the idea in 1985 to post a "Winston Million" bonus to a driver who won three of the sport's crown-jewel races: the Daytona 500, the Winston 500 at Talladega, the Coca-Cola 600 at Charlotte, and the Southern 500 at Darlington.

It was a seemingly safe bet for RJR. No one other than David Pearson and LeeRoy Yarbrough had ever won the "Big 3" before Talladega was built. And no one had come close to winning three of the four from 1969 to 1984.

Elliott came out blazing in 1985, however. With brother Ernie building engines that were far more powerful than anybody else's, Elliott's No. 9 Ford blew them away at Daytona. At Talladega, he had the most remarkable day in the history of that massive track, coming from five miles behind (almost two full laps) under green flag conditions to win it going away.

With the first $1 million payday on the line in Charlotte and the media attention kicked up, the team faltered badly, finishing 18th.

That made the Labor Day weekend race at Darlington a pressure cooker. Elliott's every step was dogged by the press and fans, so much so that two South Carolina highway patrolmen were assigned to him to keep them at bay.

"That's what I didn't want," Bill said. "Still don't. I'd rather just go out and drive the race car, deal with what I've got to deal with, load up, and go home and go to the next race."

That day, he didn't have the dominant car he had in Daytona and Talladega. In fact, he came close to going a lap down early in the race. But one by one, his competition fell by the wayside until there was only one man left to beat: Cale Yarborough. At the time, Yarborough was the only man with five Southern 500 wins, and one of the toughest competitors on the planet. But on lap 323 (of 367), smoke bellowed from beneath Yarborough's Ford, the result of a ruptured power steering line, and Elliott flew by.

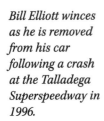

Bill Elliott winces as he is removed from his car following a crash at the Talladega Superspeedway in 1996.

He's So POP-ular

Bill Elliott has won the Most Popular Driver award, selected by fans through voting conducted by the National Motorsports Press Association, a record 16 times:

Year	Winner	Year	Winner
1952	Lee Petty	1979	David Pearson
1953	Lee Petty	1980	David Pearson
1954	Lee Petty	1981	Bobby Allison
1955	Tim Flock	1982	Bobby Allison
1956	Curtis Turner	1983	Bobby Allison
1957	Fireball Roberts	1984	Bill Elliott
1958	Jack Smith	1985	Bill Elliott
1959	Glen Wood	1986	Bill Elliott
1960	Rex White	1987	Bill Elliott
1961	Joe Weatherly	1988	Bill Elliott
1962	Richard Petty	1989	Darrell Waltrip
1963	Fred Lorenzen	1990	Darrell Waltrip
1964	Richard Petty	1991	Bill Elliott
1965	Fred Lorenzen	1992	Bill Elliott
1966	Darel Dieringer	1993	Bill Elliott
1967	Cale Yarborough	1994	Bill Elliott
1968	Richard Petty	1995	Bill Elliott
1969	Bobby Isaac	1996	Bill Elliott
1970	Richard Petty	1997	Bill Elliott
1971	Bobby Allison	1998	Bill Elliott
1972	Bobby Allison	1999	Bill Elliott
1973	Bobby Allison	2000	Bill Elliott
1974	Richard Petty	2001	Dale Earnhardt
1975	Richard Petty	2002	Bill Elliott
1976	Richard Petty	2003	Dale Earnhardt Jr.
1977	Richard Petty	2004	Dale Earnhardt Jr.
1978	Richard Petty	2005	Dale Earnhardt Jr.

"I can remember following Cale into [Turn] 3 when he blew, and I'm saying, 'Oh, no, it's going to happen again,'" Elliott said. "Fortunately, I was able to get low enough to get by him on the apron. He still gave me a run for the money, even with the broken power steering line."

The next day, Elliott's grinning face, with thousands of bogus "Million Dollar Bills" floating down around him in victory lane, was in every newspaper in the United States.

To help put Elliott's payday in perspective, the average person in 1985 with a bachelor's degree in engineering and one year's experience earned $24,100 a year. Elliott could have paid that salary for 41 years. He won $53,725 for the Southern 500 victory itself, but the additional $1 million helped him earn $2,383,186 for the year.

Success didn't destroy Bill Elliott, but it made him more wary. In spite of winning 11 races in 1985, he lost the championship to Darrell Waltrip. It would be 1988 before he claimed his only Winston Cup title.

Along the way, Elliott became the most familiar face in racing. In 19 years, he won the Most Popular Driver award 16 times. But after the death of Dale Earnhardt in 2001, he withdrew his name from the nomination. The trophy presented to the winner each year by the National Motorsports Press Association is now known as the Bill Elliott Trophy.

"Dale Earnhardt never won this award, and I think it would be a tremendous honor for the Earnhardt family to receive it this year," he said in 2001. "I certainly don't want to stand in the way of his family receiving this award."

That, noted NASCAR president Mike Helton, said more about Elliott than his 44 wins and $30 million.

"Bill's decision to step aside demonstrates just why he has been such a popular driver for so many years," Helton said. "He always puts the sport—and his fellow drivers—before himself. He's not only a great driver. He's a gentleman, too."—J.M.

Promise Unfulfilled

In a sport with a history filled with "what-ifs," there is perhaps no greater story left open-ended by fate than Tim Richmond's.

Born in Ashland, Ohio, in 1955, Richmond spent his childhood tooling around the family's farm on a go-kart and showing quarter horses. He learned how to fly an airplane before he turned 16. Because his doting mother, Evelyn, wanted only the best for her son, Richmond was sent to Miami Military Academy and excelled there in football and in track—but not necessarily in his studies. He came back to Ohio and attended college briefly, then went to work in the business owned by his father, Al, whose company made digging machines. Al Richmond wound up as the co-owner of a sprint car team that raced locally, and one night in 1976 Tim was at a race in Lakeville, Ohio, and was talked into taking the car around the track.

Tim, in the first time he'd been in a race car, turned laps that were quicker than the car's regular driver. Within weeks, Al had bought Tim a sprint car and he drove his first race at a track in Mercer, Pennsylvania. On the third lap, he spun out four times, got hit by another car, and went over a bank at the edge of the track. It was hardly an auspicious beginning to his career in motorsports.

It is an example of just how fast things happened in Richmond's life that barely four years later, in May of 1980, the same young man who'd been a whirling dervish in that sprint car in Pennsylvania was Rookie of the Year in America's premiere automobile race—the Indianapolis 500.

Richmond's car actually ran out of gas just as the race (won by Johnny Rutherford) ended. As his car coasted to a stop off the fourth turn, Richmond heard the crowd roar.

SEASON TO REMEMBER

Alan Kulwicki—1992

When fiercely independent driver-owner Alan Kulwicki finished 34th in a 36-car field at Dover in 1992, he fell behind by 278 points with just six races left in the fight for the championship. Bill Elliott led Davey Allison by 154 points at that juncture, but Elliott's team faltered and when the series went to Atlanta for the final race of the season, the championship was a dogfight.

Allison led Kulwicki by 30 points and Elliott by 40 going into the season-ending Hooters 500 at Atlanta, which also just happened to be Richard Petty's final start as a NASCAR driver. Drama hung in the air all afternoon, and as the final laps were counted off, Elliott was first with Kulwicki second. But Kulwicki had led 103 laps before making his final pit stop for a splash of gas. Elliott could only lead 102, meaning Kulwicki would get the five bonus points for leading the most laps—if he had enough fuel to make it to the end of the race.

Kulwicki, driving a Ford Thunderbird he'd nicknamed "Underbird," made it and won the championship by 10 points. If Elliott had led the most laps instead of Kulwicki, they would have tied for the title and Elliott would have been the champion based on the fact that he won more races.

"So I sort of stuck my hand up out of the car and the noise got louder," Richmond said. "I thought, 'This is neat.' So I stuck my whole arm out and the crowd went nuts. I unhooked my belts and jumped out just before it came to a complete stop. The crowd loved it and started making more noise. Now I'm standing there waving to people."

And that's when Richmond realized that while he was rolling to a stop, Rutherford had been taking his victory lap. About the time Richmond was really playing to the crowd, Rutherford rolled up behind him. Richmond, never one not to take advantage of a moment, jumped on the sidepod of Rutherford's car and rode back toward the pits with the 1980 Indianapolis 500 champion.

Evelyn Richmond wasn't a fan of Indy cars, though, and when her son escaped a dramatic wreck at Michigan later that year uninjured she put her foot down. Stock cars appeared safer, and Richmond was already looking in that direction. In July 1980, he finished 12th in his first NASCAR Winston Cup race at Pocono in a car owned by D.K. Ulrich.

NASCAR, at first, didn't know what to make of Richmond.

"One time I told my wife, 'Find out who does his hair,'" Buddy Baker once said. "'It looks better than yours.'"

Longtime *Charlotte Observer* motorsports writer Tom Higgins first saw Richmond at a press conference before a race in Charlotte. "He looked like somebody who'd stepped out of *GQ* magazine," Higgins said. "He had on a red blazer with white slacks and white shoes. His hair was perfect and he had a deep tan. He was a real dandy. I said, 'Who in God's name is this?'"

Richmond had it all, it seemed. Good looks, charisma, and a trunkload of driving talent. As he began his stock car career, fans flocked to him. Car owner Rick Hendrick, who would wind up giving Richmond his largest drink of success in the sport, has said, "Women would pee their pants when they met him, and their boyfriends would be standing there wanting Tim's autograph, too."

Richmond got a ride in 1982 with Jim Stacy's team, and that year he scored a pair of victories on the road course at Riverside, California, where he was simply a virtuoso, slinging a stock car around the right- and left-hand turns. Between 1983 and 1985, he won once at Pocono and once at North Wilkesboro while driving for a team owned by drag racer Raymond Beadle.

But it was in 1986, when Richmond joined Hendrick Motorsports, that things took off. Hendrick, a resident of Charlotte, North Carolina, who was emerging as one of the country's major auto dealers, added a second team to his NASCAR operation that year, moving veteran crew chief Harry Hyde from Geoff Bodine's team to work with Richmond.

At first, Richmond and Hyde clashed. The hotshot young driver who rode around on his Harley-Davidson motorcycle and drove every lap like he was qualifying didn't understand why Hyde kept telling him he had to take better care of his race car and his tires.

The ever-stylish Tim Richmond strikes a pose at Daytona before setting out to defend his title in the Firecracker 400.

TOP 10

Victory Leaders in NASCAR's Premier Series (1980–89)

	Driver	Wins	Races	Top 5s	Poles	Earnings
1.	Darrell Waltrip	57	296	158	41	$8,698,219
2.	Dale Earnhardt	38	296	130	4	$9,557,751
3.	Bill Elliott	32	249	97	37	$8,945,275
4.	Bobby Allison	28	251	98	6	$5,079,882
5.	Cale Yarborough	20	155	57	26	$2,243,342
6.	Rusty Wallace	16	183	50	7	$5,376,342
7.	Neil Bonnett	13t	264	66	7	$3,437,220
	Tim Richmond	13t	185	42	14	$2,310,693
9.	Terry Labonte	10t	296	105	19	$5,802,359
	Richard Petty	10t	292	65	0	$3,381,278
	Ricky Rudd	10t	278	82	16	$4,218,515

Source: www.racing-reference.info

Hyde didn't understand why the kid wouldn't listen to simple reason. After nearly coming to blows several times, they finally began to see eye-to-eye after a tire test in which Richmond ran 50 laps his way and agreed to run 50 laps Hyde's way. When Richmond saw Hyde's way was faster, a light went on.

The first race after that came at Charlotte, and Richmond finished second. He was second again the following race at Riverside, then won the race at Pocono, won the pole but finished 15th at Michigan, then won the race at Daytona. In the return trip to Pocono in July, Richmond damaged his car in a crash with less than 50 laps to go in a rain-shortened race and had to drive it in reverse halfway around the track on three flat tires. He lost a lap but made it up and beat Bodine and Ricky Rudd in a thrilling finish for another victory.

He added a win at Watkins Glen as the Cup series returned to that historic road course in New York, and then won the Southern 500 at Darlington. When he won at Richmond on September 7—

"Richmond Wins at Richmond," the headlines read—he had won six times and finished second four more times in a 12-race stretch that propelled him toward a third-place finish in the points behind Dale Earnhardt and Darrell Waltrip.

It seemed obvious to anyone watching that Richmond would be a strong contender for the championship in 1987 and for years to come after that. Many who saw him race say Richmond had as much natural ability as any driver who ever drove a stock car, and once he and Hyde got their differences ironed out they became a team to be reckoned with.

But that December, after fighting recurring colds and flu-like symptoms all fall, Richmond was diagnosed with pneumonia. But the real news was even worse. The strain of pneumonia he was suffering from had emerged as a warning sign for a new, terrible disease the medical world was just beginning to understand more about. Richmond had acquired immunodeficiency syndrome—AIDS.

Only a few people knew the diagnosis in 1987, when Richmond sat out until the Winston all-star race in May recovering from the pneumonia. He finished third in the all-star event, and then returned for his first points race at Pocono on June 14. In storybook fashion, he won. He won the next race at Riverside, too, for his 13th and final career victory.

After six more races, Richmond was unable to continue. He tried to run the season-opening Busch Clash in 1988, but NASCAR said he failed a drug test as part of a new policy it had instituted following the 1987 season. As far as anyone knows, Richmond was the only driver ever tested at that time. Shortly after saying Richmond had tested positive for "opiates," NASCAR officials admitted the results actually had shown increased levels of the medicines found in Tylenol and cold remedies. Richmond contended the test was wrong and sued NASCAR, but the case was eventually settled.

Richmond felt that NASCAR had turned its back on him, and he grew increasingly isolated from even his closest friends in the sport. He was injured in a fall from a motorcycle in early 1989, and over that summer his health deteriorated.

TOP 10

Racing Movies

Days of Thunder, loosely based on the lives of Tim Richmond and Harry Hyde, is not the only movie involving stock-car racing. Here are 10 significant, if not critically acclaimed, movies with stock-car racing figuring into the plot, listed in order of release:

1. *Thunder in Carolina* (1960)
2. *Red Line 7000* (1965)
3. *Fireball 500* (1966)
4. *Speedway* (1968)
5. *43: The Petty Story* (1972)
6. *The Last American Hero* (1973)
7. *Greased Lightning* (1977)
8. *Six Pack* (1982)
9. *Stroker Ace* (1983)
10. *Days of Thunder* (1990)

On the morning of August 13, a Sunday when the Winston Cup circuit was back at Watkins Glen where Richmond had won during his magical streak just two years earlier, Richmond passed away.

Richmond, said his friend Kyle Petty, was trapped in time.

"He could have raced against my grandfather and been right at home in those days," Petty said, referring to NASCAR pioneer Lee Petty, one of the sport's earliest stars. "And today, he wouldn't stick out at all.

"Jeff Gordon has a place to stay when he goes to New York. Tim beat him there by about 25 years. NASCAR has an office in Los Angeles because it wants to be a factor in Hollywood. Tim beat them there by 20 years. He was going everyplace that NASCAR would eventually go.... He was way out ahead of everyone, and his racing backed up everything he was doing."

Richmond wanted to become an actor and was scheduled for a screen test in California on a trip there in late 1986. He missed that test, though, because of a doctor's visit. The 1990 movie *Days of Thunder* was largely based on the lives of Richmond and Harry Hyde.

"I am not sure Dale Earnhardt would have dominated the sport the way he did if Tim had been around," Petty said. "Richmond had more talent in his little finger than a lot of us ever had, period. All it needed to be was harnessed and honed."

The first time Hendrick saw Jeff Gordon driving a car, in a Busch Series race in Atlanta in early 1992, he said it reminded him of how Richmond drove.

"There's no question in my mind Tim would have won championships," Hendrick said.

Had Richmond still been alive and driving for Hendrick, would the man who would eventually help Gordon win four championships have noticed the youngster at all?

What if?

It's a question that can never be answered.—D.P.

Two's Company, Three's a Crowd, and Four's a Team

Dale Jarrett was driving for Robert Yates Racing in the 1995 NASCAR Winston Cup season after Ernie Irvan, who had been driving the team's No. 28 Fords, was seriously injured in a crash the year before at Michigan.

Irvan was making miraculous progress in his recovery, however, and it was clear that he'd eventually be coming back. Jarrett knew that likely meant he'd soon have to find another place to drive because he knew how Yates felt about the idea of a multi-car team.

"Kelley [Jarrett's wife] and I were riding in the car with Robert at Indianapolis one day," Jarrett recalled. "Robert said, 'You know, I don't think two teams would ever work for me. They can't make victory lane big enough for two cars, so somebody is always going to be disappointed.'"

Today, just more than a decade after that conversation, that kind of thinking could not be less conventional in NASCAR's top series.

From the beginning of that 1995 season through early September 2006, 400 Cup races have been held. Teams owned by two men—Rick Hendrick and Jack Roush—won 189 of those races. Add the multicar teams owned by Joe Gibbs, Richard Childress, Yates, Roger Penske, and Dale and Teresa Earnhardt, and that ratio is 352 of 400 races.

The last time a driver for a single-car team won a Cup race was Ricky Craven in a victory at Darlington Raceway in March 2003.

Throughout NASCAR history, the pendulum has swung a number of times between the prevalence of single- and multicar

One measure of a car owner's long-term success is the number of different drivers with which a team has won races? The Wood Brothers lead that list, with 16 winners.

DID YOU KNOW . . .

Wood Brothers	16
Hendrick Motorsports	11
Holman-Moody	10†
Junior Johnson	10†
Bud Moore	9
Petty Enterprises	8

teams. But never before has the swing in either direction gone as far as it has toward big teams these days.

In 2005, NASCAR officials announced they would impose a limit of four teams for any one car owner. While that was seen as a way to rein in Roush, who put all five of the Cup teams he owned into the Chase for the Nextel Cup, NASCAR also said Roush would be allowed to fulfill existing relationships with his sponsors, so at the end of 2006, Roush was still the owner of five teams.

Hendrick, meanwhile, fields four teams. Gibbs, Childress, Ray Evernham, and Chip Ganassi each had three, while Dale Earnhardt Inc. plans to go from two to three teams in 2007. Penske had three teams in 2005, but went back to two in 2006. Yates has two teams, as do Ginn Motorsports and Petty Enterprises. Michael Waltrip plans to field three Toyota teams in 2007, with Bill Davis and Red Bull Racing having two each.

How much room in a 43-car field does that leave for anyone else? Not much.

The modern NASCAR economy simply makes it difficult to field a competitive single-car team. If a four-car team can sign primary and associate sponsorship deals averaging $10 million per year per car—and that's conservative—that's $40 million to spend on racing. And those four teams can share many resources—million-dollar machinery and engineering staff to apply what those machines can do to help race cars go faster, for example—that a single-car team also must have in order to compete.

Even though NASCAR changed its rules in 2006, limiting the number of times each team can go to tracks where the Cup series

TRIVIA

Cars carrying No. 43, thanks to Richard Petty, have won 198 races in Cup racing. That's more than any other number. Which number is second on that list?

Answers to the trivia questions are on pages 180–181.

runs to test, a four-car team can still try things at those tests four times faster than a single-car team. In a sport where the difference between running up front and running in the back of the pack can be as slim as a half-second a lap, there's no way to overestimate the importance of having multiple chances to figure out what might work and what most likely will not before the cars even show up at the track.

Money, of course, has almost always equaled speed in NASCAR and any other form of racing. In the second season of what's now the Nextel Cup Series, the champion was part of a two-car team. Bill Rexford won the title that season in cars owned by Julian Buesink, with Lloyd Moore driving the other team's car.

Brothers Tim and Bob Flock both drove for Ted Chester in 1951 and 1952, and then were part of the sport's first true superteam with owner Carl Kiekhaefer in 1955 and 1956. In 1956 alone, Kiekhaefer-owned cars won 30 races and a championship with Buck Baker.

Throughout the sport's history, several teams have won with different drivers and entered multiple cars in the same race. The all-time roster of drivers for teams like the Wood Brothers and the Ford factory–backed Holman-Moody team reads like a who's who of the sport's history.

But the formula for making more than one team work well together remained elusive. Junior Johnson ran a two-car team with Darrell Waltrip and Neil Bonnett from 1984 to 1986 and tells the story about how he'd go back and forth between the teams' separate shops telling them that the other team was working on something really special for the next week's race, figuring that was the best way to drain every drop of performance from both.

Hendrick went from one to two cars in 1986, just the third year of his team's existence. He had two very different crew chiefs in hotshot young guy Gary Nelson and grizzled veteran Harry Hyde, with Nelson working with Geoffrey Bodine and Hyde with Tim Richmond's team.

"Gary and Bodine were both innovative, and they had some stuff on their cars I thought might work on Tim's car," Hendrick recalled. "But I knew I couldn't just tell Harry he needed to do it."

So Hendrick arranged to take Hyde into Nelson's shop late one night, giving Hyde a peek at Nelson's cars. Just as Hendrick expected, Hyde dismissed the things Nelson was trying as gimmicks. But, also as Hendrick expected, some of those gimmicks started showing up on the cars Hyde was building for Richmond soon thereafter.

A decade later, Hendrick dealt with the ultimate test of team-mates when two of his drivers wound up battling each other for the championship. Terry Labonte won the 1996 title with Jeff Gordon finishing second, and although the teams had worked together to some degree that season, there was very little of that going on as they fought for first near the season's end.

"[Crew chief] Ray [Evernham] felt like we were coming up with all of that good stuff, so why would we want to share it?" Gordon said. "We wanted to take that advantage and hold on to it. It doesn't make sense, really. You work so hard to get something and then you just give it away. When

Rick Hendrick scouts out the garage area at New Hampshire International Speedway prior to a race in September 2006.

you find something that's really working, it's still hard if you feel like you're giving and giving and giving and not getting anything in return.

"But your teammates are working as well, and they might find something in another area that you might need some day. The return is coming, you just don't know when."

Over the past decade, the statistics show that Hendrick and Roush have figured out a lot about expanding teamwork beyond one car number to include their much broader organizations, which now each employ somewhere around 500 people.

They bring very different approaches to the task.

"I like to operate a debate of people who're very talented with more experience and better judgment than I have," Roush said.

Jack Roush put all five of his teams into the 2005 Chase for the Nextel Cup.
Photo courtesy of David Durochik/SportPics.

"Without that kind of debate, I don't think you get to things people would rather not talk about and you have trouble finding out where the strengths and weaknesses are. Rick might be too nice of a guy to do that."

Hendrick grew up around race cars and actually drove in two Cup races himself early in his team's history. But he's far less hands-on around the track than Roush.

TRIVIA

What is the historical significance of Fred Lorenzen's victory at Augusta Speedway on September 13, 1962?

Answers to the trivia questions are on pages 180–181.

"I love cars and I love to drive. I love to work on them," Hendrick said. "But am I a better salesman than I am a machinist or a tuner? You find your niche. I can hire smarter guys who can do those things and hold those people accountable for the competition side. I do feel like I am better at the marketing side. With all the sponsors we have, I am out there hugging and kissing on them and raising money because about 80 percent of what we have comes from them."

For Roush, getting all five of his teams in the 2005 Chase is a great accomplishment.

"The thing I would credit my team for is having mutual respect," Roush said. "If you have one guy who rejects the others, or if the others reject one guy, then you have a dysfunctional team.

"I have people who believe in and approve of their contemporaries. That's pretty special. I don't expect to keep that going forward to the extent we've got it today. I will be amazed if we don't lose it over a period of time. But that is what we have worked toward."

Evernham has his own multicar team now, and he looks back on how things were when he was Gordon's crew chief in a different time.

"We fought like cats and dogs," Evernham said. "I am sorry for everything I did because now I understand. I feel like I owe them a ton of apologies for some of the stuff I said and did worrying about my own little projects. They did a phenomenal job keeping that going. But I also would bet if you ask Jack and Rick, that's still their toughest challenge, keeping the teamwork going."

DID YOU KNOW ...

In the second race of the 2006 Nextel Cup season, Tony Stewart finished 43rd, last place, and won $131,453. Rookie Denny Hamlin, on the other hand, finished 12th and won $94,575. How can this be?

The answer is fairly complicated, but the short version is that Stewart is eligible for several bonus and contingency plans that pad his winnings for each race. For example, Stewart's team gets part of the money from television rights paid into what's called an "owner's plan" for each race. Hamlin, who is Stewart's Joe Gibbs Racing teammate, isn't on that plan.

Stewart is also part of a "winner's circle" plan that pays an amount for each race he enters because he was among those who won races in 2005.

If you look closely at the sides of Nextel Cup cars, you will see several stickers affixed. Each of these stickers represents a contingency plan that each car may or may not be taking part in. The more stickers, as a general rule, the more money that car will make in a given race.

Determination to keep it going, at least until another NASCAR trend comes along, might be the key.

"You grow your folks with the same philosophy and it becomes a situation where it's not my philosophy, it's theirs," Hendrick said. "It's all of us, together, making decisions, saying, 'This is how we're going to do it.'

"You can't sink half of a ship. If you mess up one of your teams, it's going to affect the others. It's to everybody's advantage for us to make the right decisions. I think everybody has bought into that."

Finally.—D.P.

A Clean Break

There is a compelling, almost visceral, tug on an athlete to stay beyond his time. Money problems caused the great Joe Louis to hang on long after his boxing skills had eroded. Joe Namath played on knees hardly suitable for walking, much less pro football.

In racing, the last of a generation of diehard drivers struggled with that decision in 2005. Two-time champion Terry Labonte cut back from a full-time schedule in 2005, but didn't quit racing entirely. Mark Martin said he was quitting after 2004, then gave team owner Jack Roush one more year.

Rusty Wallace, however, walked away clean.

"I guess if my car owner came to me and said, 'You need to help us,' I'd have to say, 'I wish I could but I can't,'" Wallace said on the evening of his final race, at Homestead-Miami Speedway in 2005.

But then, even Wallace hedged his bet.

"If the new driver went out there and something went wrong and he got hurt, if he got hurt, got in a crash or something, and they called me up and said, 'Rusty, can you fill in for four or five races?' then absolutely, I'd do that."

When you've been racing your whole life, the sport's pull is strong. But for Wallace, the desire not to hang around too long was even stronger. He wanted to go out on top, and he did that.

In 1980, Wallace began his career in NASCAR's top division spectacularly, taking a one-shot deal from Roger Penske, a man who would later play a huge part in his career, and turning it into a second-place finish in Atlanta.

Over the next 25 years, Wallace posted 55 wins, good for eighth place on the all-time win list. In 1989, driving for drag racer

Rusty Wallace's 55 career wins puts him in eighth place on the all-time list.
Photo courtesy of David Durochik/SportPics.

Raymond Beadle's Winston Cup team, he won his only Cup Series championship, by a 12-point margin over his old pal Dale Earnhardt.

He also finished second twice in the championship standings, to Bill Elliott by a mere 24 points in 1988, and to Earnhardt in 1993. From 1986 to 2001, Wallace won at least one race every season, and his 17 finishes in the top 10 in the points standings (including 10 straight from 1993 to 2002) is tied for sixth place, all-time.

When Penske, the open-wheel king, decided to turn his attention to stock cars, he hired Wallace as the first driver for his Penske South Racing team, and eventually Wallace got a piece of the ownership pie.

Wallace's two biggest seasons would come at the wheel of the No. 2 car owned by Penske, when he won 10 races in 1993 and eight in 1994. Thirty-four of Wallace's Winston Cup wins came as Penske's driver.

Among all his stats, however, the most important one to him might be the last one he posted. Although he didn't win the championship in 2005, he qualified for the 10-man Chase for the Nextel Cup. He finished eighth in the final standings, but at least he made the cut. To a man with pride, that counted.

"When you quit full-time racing...you would hope that you go out on top of your game," he said. "That's the reason I retired when I did from racing."

Wallace was one of the last of the old-time racers who knew as much about how to work on his car as he did how to drive it. He worked on cars his entire career. And in the end, when the sport became so sophisticated that it required mechanical engineers to keep up with the technology, it may have hurt him. But he was always the man to call the shots.

"There are many, many drivers that pop up right now and go, 'Hey, I'm a great driver,'" Wallace said. "I'm like, 'Oh yeah, can you build a shock? Can you work on a car?' I don't have much respect for drivers that don't know how to work on their cars or that aren't hands-on."

Like any other driver who made it to the top, Wallace had his share of run-ins with other drivers. In the 1985 Goody's 500 at Bristol, Earnhardt and Wallace tangled, knocking Wallace out of contention. Wallace confronted Earnhardt while Earnhardt was

SEASON TO REMEMBER

Rusty Wallace—1993

Rusty Wallace won a Winston Cup title in 1996, but he won the most races in his career in 1993 while driving for Roger Penske. Nine of Wallace's 10 victories in a 30-race schedule had something in common, too. The first nine came on tracks either right at one mile long—Rockingham and New Hampshire—or shorter. It wasn't until the final race of the season, at Atlanta, where Wallace won a race on an intermediate-style track.

TOP 10

Leaders in Second-Place Finishes*

1.	Richard Petty	157
2.	David Pearson	89
3.	Bobby Allison	87
4.	Dale Earnhardt	70
5.	Cale Yarborough	59
6.	Darrell Waltrip	58
7.	Buck Baker	56
8.	Mark Martin	53
9.	Lee Petty	48
10.	Buddy Baker	42 t
	Terry Labonte	42 t
	Rusty Wallace	42 t

* Through the 2005 season.

Source: www.racing-reference.info

engaged in a TV interview, and angrily bounced a water bottle off his nose.

"I wasn't going to stay mad at Dale," Wallace said, "but I needed to let him know how I felt at that moment."

In his championship season, Wallace knocked Darrell Waltrip out on his way to victory lane in the All-Star race, the Winston, and the tables completely turned. Up until then, Waltrip was the racer they all loved to hate and Wallace was on his way to being one of the most popular champions in the sport's history.

"I don't think there has ever been, in the history of our sport, a situation where in a split second the roles are reversed like that—totally reversed," Wallace said.

For the remainder of that season, Wallace got the boos that were normally reserved for Waltrip. Characteristically, though, he attacked the problem head-on. He handled the boos with grace and consciously set out to repair the PR damage.

"That wreck cost me a ton of fans," he said. "I'm going to do whatever it takes to get them back. I don't care how many public appearances or whatever I have to make, I'm going to do them."

When Wallace hung up his driving shoes, driving was the only thing he gave up. He went to work as a race analyst for ESPN/ABC in the Indy Racing League, with an eye to return to NASCAR along with those networks in 2007.

He attends to his car dealerships and keeps his finger in the pie at Penske South. But he also works with building his Busch Series team, grooming his son Steven to take over the ride in 2007.

"I'll be involved in the sport," he said. "I'll always be involved in the sport and be competitive."—J.M.

Brother to Brother

There's a photo from victory lane after the 1996 NAPA 500 at Atlanta Motor Speedway that, a hundred years from now, would give a historian pause. There, right in the middle of the postrace celebration, are two guys, both holding up their index fingers.

What? Two number ones?

"That was way cool," said Bobby Labonte, the race winner that chilly November day. "There in victory lane were Rick Hendrick, Joe Gibbs, Terry and I, and Mom and Dad. I look at that picture quite a bit. It was a monumental day. Our parents won twice that day—their kids won both deals."

It was a moment unique in any sport, to have siblings celebrating together, one for winning the battle and the other for winning the war. Even in a sport such as NASCAR racing, which has historically pitted brother against brother and occasionally father against son, never had such a moment arrived.

Terry Labonte, the older of Bob and Martha Labonte's racing sons from Corpus Christi, Texas, claimed his second NASCAR Winston Cup championship that afternoon with a steady fifth-place finish in the race, driving for car owner Rick Hendrick. "The Iceman" won his second championship with the same smooth, unflappable driving style with which he'd won his first. It was almost 12 years to the day after he wrapped up his first title.

On that same day, Bobby, seven years younger than Terry, won the race to sweeten what for him and his car owner, former Washington Redskins coach Joe Gibbs, had been a bad season. The win was the only one Bobby had in 1996. He finished 11th in the points standings.

It was another four years before Bobby won his own Winston Cup championship, giving the Labonte brothers another distinction: the only brothers in NASCAR history to both become champions.

If Bobby's crown in 2000 was coming full circle for him, then the 1996 victory lane celebration was at least three-quarters of a lap. He'd been there for his brother's first race and first win, and then co-celebrated his final championship.

At Darlington Raceway, a pivotal track in Terry Labonte's career, Bobby was a tagalong for his big brother's first Winston Cup race in 1978. His stature hadn't risen very much when Terry took his first victory, in the 1980 Southern 500.

"I just came down as a little brother. I was in the way," Bobby said. "I snuck in the garage area and snuck into the pits. In '80, I know I was on pit road because I went to victory lane. Darrell Bryant was the crew chief and Terry ended up winning it when the three leaders all crashed on the last lap and Terry beat David Pearson back to the line by a fender.

Bobby Labonte, seven years younger than his brother Terry, gave the family its third Winston Cup championship in 2000. Photo courtesy of David Durochik/SportPics.

TOP 10

Oldest Drivers to Win a Cup Race*

	Driver	Date	Track	Age
1.	Harry Gant	9/6/92	Michigan	52 years, 7 months, 6 days
2.	Morgan Shepherd	3/20/93	Atlanta	51 years, 4 months, 27 days
3.	Bobby Allison	2/14/88	Daytona	50 years, 2 months, 11 days
4.	Dale Earnhardt	10/15/00	Talladega	49 years, 5 months, 16 days
5.	Dale Jarrett	10/2/05	Talladega	48 years, 10 months, 6 days
6.	Bill Elliott	11/9/03	Rockingham	48 years, 1 month, 1 day
7.	Rusty Wallace	4/18/04	Martinsville	47 years, 8 months, 4 days
8.	Geoffrey Bodine	8/11/96	Watkins Glen	47 years, 3 months, 24 days
9.	Richard Petty	7/4/84	Daytona	47 years, 2 days
10.	Terry Labonte	8/31/03	Darlington	46 years, 9 months, 15 days

* As of August 31, 2006.

Source: NASCAR Statistical Services

"It was pretty exciting for Terry because he was awfully young. I was 16, and didn't exactly know what was going on, but it was definitely exciting."

Bobby would bring his own excitement to the family in his career, which continues with him now driving the famed No. 43 Dodges for the Petty Enterprises team. He got his first win driving for the Gibbs-owned team in the Coca-Cola 600 at Charlotte in 1995, but seemed to have a particular knack for winning at Atlanta Motor Speedway, where he has six of his 21 career victories. He was particularly successful in the track's second race each year, winning it four times between that memorable day in 1996 and 2001.

For Terry, it was a 26-year journey before he announced his "Gearing Down" retirement tour at the end of 2004. In 2005–06, Labonte ran only select races in order to devote more time to his family, in particular to the racing career of his son Justin. With 22 wins and two titles, he had very little left to prove.

Terry broke Richard Petty's record of 513 consecutive starts in 1996 and continued his "Iron Man" streak until August 5, 2000, when he missed the Brickyard 400 at Indianapolis while recovering from injuries suffered a month earlier in the Pepsi 400 at Daytona Beach.

DID YOU KNOW . . . From the day Rudd stepped into his first full-time ride in 1981 until the day he hung up his helmet after the 2004 Nextel Cup season, Rudd raced in an incredible 788 consecutive races? Along the way, he passed such notables as Richard Petty (513) and the man who broke Petty's record, Terry "the Iceman" Labonte (655).

That's nice, but a number Rudd likes better is 16. That's the number of consecutive years in which he won at least one race. It tied him with Darrell Waltrip and left him one year shy of Richard Petty's all-time mark.

"I kind of couple the two together," Rudd said. "To be out here every weekend, that says one thing, but to have that win streak, that kind of goes hand in hand with it."

Labonte's record mark of 655 consecutive starts was topped in 2002 by Ricky Rudd.

Terry had driven with broken bones before; indeed, in that 1996 photo his left hand was in a cast after he broke it at Phoenix. But when he took himself out of the game for the Brickyard 400, it was for something potentially career-threatening that turned out to be nothing but an inner-ear problem that was misdiagnosed.

"We were all getting very nervous, very concerned, and yeah, I thought about it [Labonte not being able to drive again]," said Gary DeHart, his crew chief. "I said, 'Gosh darn, this just can't be happening like this. It could be something that's permanent and he'll never drive again.' We didn't talk about it, but the thought was always there."

"I got dizzy," Labonte said. "That's when we went to a different ear doctor and they diagnosed me with benign paroxysmal positional vertigo. They did some therapy for it, and I haven't had a problem since. If it had been diagnosed correctly the first time, I'd have never missed a race or a practice."

If there was an affinity between the racing Labonte brothers beyond sharing cool hands behind a steering wheel, it was a mutual affection for Darlington. Terry's career began there and had gotten its first big boost there. In 2000, Bobby added his name to the list of Southern 500 winners.

In what turned out to be an appropriate swan song, Terry won the Southern 500 again in 2003, the last time that race was run on Labor Day weekend. That was his full circle.

"I remember when I won that [first] race, they sent me a set of glasses that had all the names of the winners on it," Terry said. "I don't know if they still do it anymore, but it had all the names, Buck Baker, Curtis Turner, a bunch of them. I looked at all the names and there was my name, I believe, right beside David Pearson's. I thought, 'That's pretty cool.'"—J.M.

Making His Mark

Mark Martin called the 2005 Nextel Cup season his "My Salute to You" farewell Nextel Cup tour, and it turned out to be a long good-bye.

During that season, after which Martin planned to leave full-time Nextel Cup competition, sponsorship and other issues put team owner Jack Roush in a bind. He needed another season out of Martin in the No. 6 Fords.

Martin, determined more than anything else to go out of NASCAR's top circuit with his competitive dignity intact, would never have said yes for anyone else. But he also could not say no to the man with whom he had enjoyed so much success. So Martin returned in 2006 for one more season, his 19th at Roush Racing, proving not only the bonds of loyalty between driver and car owner but also the fact that they have made a formidable team.

"Mark and I struggled often and mightily in the early days," Roush said. "But Mark always came to my side whenever the team's long-term interests were threatened."

Martin has stepped out of full-time Nextel Cup competition for 2007. He will share a ride with Regan Smith at Ginn Racing.

All along, as he has talked about phasing out of the Cup series, Martin has distanced himself from the concept of retirement.

No matter when he finally does hang up the helmet, Martin has come a long way since his series debut in 1981, when he drove his own car. That deal went bad because a sponsor failed to hold up its end of the bargain, and for a while it looked as if he would be headed back to his hometown of Batesville, Arkansas, with his tail between his legs. But after hooking up with Roush in 1988, on October 22,

1989, he got his first Cup victory, at Rockingham, North Carolina, and things began to click.

Martin went into the 2006 season with 35 career victories, and he has finished outside the top 10 in points only twice since then. Going into the 2006 Chase for the Nextel Cup, he had 12 top-five points finishes, including four runner-up finishes. Martin, his Roush teammate Matt Kenseth, and Jimmie Johnson are the only three drivers who've made the Chase in each of the first three years that format has existed.

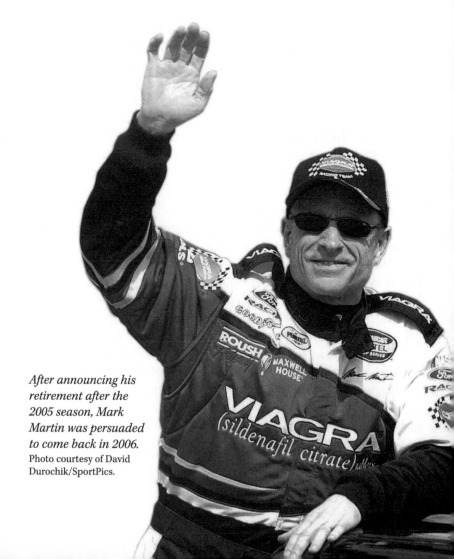

After announcing his retirement after the 2005 season, Mark Martin was persuaded to come back in 2006. Photo courtesy of David Durochik/SportPics.

Keep on
Truckin'

Since NASCAR began its Craftsman Truck Series in 1995, the series has continued to gain popularity and provide both a proving ground for young drivers and a place where veteran drivers can go to compete outside of Nextel Cup. Here's a look at the drivers who've won the Truck Series championship and Rookie of the Year awards:

Year	Champion	Rookie of the Year
1995	Mike Skinner	None
1996	Ron Hornaday Jr.	Bryan Reffner
1997	Jack Sprague	Kenny Irwin Jr.
1998	Ron Hornaday Jr.	Greg Biffle
1999	Jack Sprague	Mike Stefanik
2000	Greg Biffle	Kurt Busch
2001	Jack Sprague	Travis Kvapil
2002	Mike Bliss	Brendan Gaughan
2003	Travis Kvapil	Carl Edwards
2004	Bobby Hamilton	David Reutimann
2005	Ted Musgrave	Todd Kluever

Source: www.racing-reference.info

Not bad for a self-described "little hillbilly from Arkansas" who learned to drive, not at, but *on* his daddy's knee.

Julian Martin taught his son to drive by holding him in his lap and tearing up the back roads, with Mark alternately scared to death and giggling with delight. That love for speed was translated to the track even before he was old enough for a driver's license.

Martin was the 1974 Arkansas state champion, and in 1977 he moved over to the Midwestern American Speed Association, where he took Rookie of the Year honors. He followed that with ASA titles from 1978 to 1980 and another ASA championship in 1986.

Martin made a splash on NASCAR's Busch Series in 1987 when he had three wins, five top-fives and 13 top-10s in 27 races. He never drove a full Busch schedule after he moved up to the Winston Cup in 1988, but he holds the Busch Series record with 47 wins and is tied for the most poles, with 28.

Before the turn of the 21st century, the Busch division evolved from a "golf game" series for double-dipping Cup drivers to one in

Busch's
Best

When NASCAR dropped tracks of less than a half-mile in length from the schedule, it created a Late Model Sportsman division for racers not quite ready for the bigger Cup tracks. By 1982, that had evolved into the Busch Series, in which Mark Martin is the all-time race winner but has never won the championship. Here are the champions and Rookie of the Year award winners in Busch Series history:

Year	Champion	Rookie of the Year
1982	Jack Ingram	None
1983	Sam Ard	None
1984	Sam Ard	None
1985	Jack Ingram	None
1986	Larry Pearson	None
1987	Larry Pearson	None
1988	Tommy Ellis	None
1989	Rob Moroso	Kenny Wallace
1990	Chuck Bown	Joe Nemechek
1991	Bobby Labonte	Jeff Gordon
1992	Joe Nemechek	Ricky Craven
1993	Steve Grissom	Hermie Sadler
1994	David Green	Johnny Benson
1995	Johnny Benson	Jeff Fuller
1996	Randy LaJoie	Glen Allen Jr.
1997	Randy LaJoie	Steve Park
1998	Dale Earnhardt Jr.	Andy Santerre
1999	Dale Earnhardt Jr.	Tony Raines
2000	Jeff Green	Kevin Harvick
2001	Kevin Harvick	Greg Biffle
2002	Greg Biffle	Scott Riggs
2003	Brian Vickers	David Stremme
2004	Martin Truex Jr.	Kyle Busch
2005	Martin Truex Jr.	Carl Edwards

Source: www.racing-reference.info

which a third of the field that raced on Saturdays used that day as a tune-up for the Cup race on Sundays. It says something about Martin's makeup that he never viewed it like that. The Busch races were just as important to him as the rest, and they got the same effort as his Cup races.

"I could never just say, 'Aw, it's almost over with, it don't matter,'" Martin once said. "'Forget happy hour, I'll go out and make a few laps and park that thing.' I bleed for it. I'll bleed for that win because that's what I do and that's the kind of person that I am."

If that doesn't say it all, consider this: in the International Race of Champions, Martin also holds the record for most titles (five) and race wins (13). The IROC series pits drivers from several racing disciplines against each other in identically prepared cars. It's all driver, and the mano-a-mano aspect of it is right up his alley.

"Mark Martin is a racer's racer," Rusty Wallace, the 1989 Winston Cup champion, once said. The two raced each other all the way from the ASA through the Winston Cup, and Wallace said that nothing had changed about his old foe and friend.

"He has been a consistently class act," Wallace said. "The thing that stands out about him is his determination. He'll run the damn tires off his car and then race you on the rims."

Martin went into the 2006 Chase still looking for his first career championship, but the fact that he has not won a title has always seemed to bother others considerably more than it has Martin.

The first time he finished second, in 1990, he lost by 26 points to Dale Earnhardt after earlier that year being hit with a 46-point penalty by NACSAR that, to this day, Martin and Roush feel was undeserved. But Martin doesn't spend a whole lot of time worrying about what might have been.

"I'm not owed a championship. I'm just not owed one," he said. "I don't think I have one coming to me. If I can go earn it, then I'll get one. When I look at Dale Jarrett or Bobby Labonte or Terry Labonte or Bill Elliott, I don't look at them differently because they've got that trophy. They are what they are in my eyes because of what they did on the racetrack, not because of the trophy that they got. That's the best way I can put it. I'm not going to shed a tear because I didn't win something that I didn't earn."

Perfect? No—But Still a Wonder

Jeff Gordon never claimed to be perfect.

Still, there are large numbers of NASCAR fans who go to the track every week with the express intent of cheering for their favorite driver and booing lustily at any mention of Gordon.

He's too good to be true, his detractors claim. He never had to pay his dues the way champions of earlier generations did. He got too much, too fast. He had to be cheating, or NASCAR was "giving" him the success to groom the clean-cut, California-born lad who moved to Indiana as a teenager so he could race more into a marketable superstar.

And then, when his marriage to a former Miss Winston failed and he went through what turned into a fairly messy divorce, many of the same people who hated him and his first wife, Brooke, for being "Ken and Barbie" turned things around and tried to pretend as though Gordon wasn't allowed to have human frailties.

"There is no doubt there are more eyes and more ears on you," Gordon said of the stature he's attained in winning four championships, 75 races, and more money than any driver in NASCAR history. "I certainly recognize that and I am comfortable with it. If I wasn't, I would retire right now. I would go hide out somewhere and nobody would ever hear from me again."

For all of the challenges Gordon faces, at least one fellow NASCAR champion thinks Gordon is on the money most all the time.

"I admire Jeff so much," Tony Stewart said. "He gets it right every time. No matter the situation, it seems like he handles it exactly the right way."

For his entire career, it seems all eyes have been on California-born Jeff Gordon. Photo courtesy of David Durochik/SportPics.

It is easy to forget that Gordon is only 35 years old. He ran his first Cup race in the finale of the 1992 season, which also happened to be Richard Petty's last race, at the age of 21. While that is not quite as uncommon in today's era of "young guns," it was exceedingly rare when Gordon first came to NASCAR's top series. But then again, there has rarely been anything ordinary about what Gordon has done in his career and can do in a race car.

Born in Vallejo, California, Gordon was barely three months old when his mother and father divorced. About the time Jeff turned one year old, his mother, Carol, decided to go on a date with a man who worked at the same company she did. His name was John Bickford, and they went to Vallejo Speedway with Jeff and his sister, Kim, tagging along.

SEASON TO REMEMBER

Jeff Gordon—1998

A year that began with Dale Earnhardt finally getting his first Daytona 500 victory ended with Jeff Gordon claiming his third championship in four years and matching Richard Petty's modern-era record with 13 race victories in a season. Gordon won the Coca-Cola 600 at Charlotte, the Brickyard 400 at Indianapolis, and the Southern 500 at Darlington. He also swept both of the season's road-course events and finished with a flourish, winning three of the year's final four events to match Petty's mark from 1975.

By the time Jeff was four, Bickford was his stepfather and his partner in trying to convince Carol to let the young boy stretch his wings. Jeff wanted to race BMX bicycles, but Carol said no. Somehow, though, Jeff and Bickford convinced her that it would be safer to race a quarter-midget car. Gordon's first laps in a race car were turned in a field at the Vallejo fairgrounds, after Bickford had clipped down some weeds.

By age eight, Gordon had won his first quarter-midget national title. He kept right on winning, but eventually he reached a point where he'd done all there was to do in the quarter-midget cars.

Gordon had raced all over the country, and he and Bickford knew that Jeff could move up to sprint cars at age 14 if they moved to Indiana. They moved to Pittsboro, Indiana, and Gordon spent his days going to high school and his nights going all over that open-wheel crazy state making a name for himself. By the time he graduated, he had won more than 100 races.

Gordon was becoming something of a national sensation by appearing in sprint-car races televised by ESPN, and it was a story for the cable network that diverted him from an almost certain path toward Indy Car racing. In 1990, ESPN arranged to send him to North Carolina Speedway in Rockingham to drive a stock car for the first time at Buck Baker's driving school. His mother had to come, too, because Jeff wasn't yet old enough to rent the car he'd need to drive to the track from the airport.

Legend has it that at some point during that test at Rockingham, Gordon made a phone call to Bickford and said, "This is it. This is what I want to do."

Whether that happened or not, fate intersected with opportunity that day. Another driver at the track that day was Hugh Connerty, who wanted to drive in some Busch Series races later that year. But when he saw Gordon, he decided to hire the young man from the Midwest instead. Connerty was related to NASCAR team owner Leo Jackson, whose crew chief was Andy Petree. And Petree knew a guy who might be interested in working with the young driver. His name was Ray Evernham.

Gordon spent two seasons in the Busch Series, learning how to handle a stock car the hard way. Finally, in March of 1992, he got his first Busch victory at Atlanta Motor Speedway driving a Ford owned by Bill Davis.

That day, another car owner was walking out of a tunnel under the track toward some suites when he saw Gordon's No. 1 car go by.

"I got up to the suite and I told them, 'Watch that guy in the No. 1 car, because he's getting ready to bust his butt,'" Rick Hendrick said. "But he didn't. He won the race."

The next week, Hendrick was talking about what he saw in his office when Andy Graves, a Hendrick Motorsports employee, was within earshot. Graves happened to be sharing an apartment with Gordon, and he knew that despite what everyone believed, Gordon did not have a contract beyond the end of the 1992 Busch Series season. Within weeks, Hendrick had signed Gordon to drive for him as a rookie in 1993, hiring Evernham as the crew chief for the No. 24 Chevrolets. Those certainly were two of the better hires in Hendrick's great NASCAR career.

Over nearly seven seasons together, Gordon and Evernham built an incredible chemistry between themselves and their "Rainbow Warriors" crew—so named for the colorful paint job on the team's Chevrolets. That paid off with three championships and 47 Cup victories before Evernham left near the end of the 1999 season to pursue ownership of his own team.

TOP 10

Drivers on the All-Time Career Earnings List*

1.	Jeff Gordon	$74,895,269
2.	Mark Martin	$53,880,912
3.	Dale Jarrett	$52,303,858
4.	Rusty Wallace	$49,736,138
5.	Tony Stewart	$48,478,329
6.	Bobby Labonte	$45,690,661
7.	Dale Earnhardt	$41,999,272
8.	Ricky Rudd	$40,836,370
9.	Jeff Burton	$40,458,341
10.	Terry Labonte	$39,131,776

* Through the 2005 season.

Source: www.racing-reference.info

From 1995 through 1998, Gordon ran in 127 races and won 40 of them. He finished in the top 10 in 98 of those starts, and in the 1998 season he won a remarkable 13 times, tying Richard Petty's modern-era record.

Evernham's departure broke up one of the great teams in the sport's history, but Gordon was a long way from finished. In fact, he won the two races immediately following Evernham's departure from the team, as though signaling the other drivers that his party wasn't over. He has won four times at Indianapolis, including the inaugural Brickyard 400 in 1994. He has won the Daytona 500 three times and is a five-time winner of the Southern 500 at Darlington Raceway. He added a fourth championship in 2001 with Robbie Loomis as his crew chief, and when Gordon won at Chicagoland Speedway in July of 2006 it was his 75th career win—just one short of tying the legendary Dale Earnhardt.

Earnhardt is generally credited with hanging the nickname "Wonder Boy" on Gordon when he first appeared on the NASCAR scene. At the New York City banquet honoring Gordon's first title in

1995, Gordon saluted his rival with a toast of milk after Earnhardt had said Gordon wasn't old enough to drink champagne.

While Earnhardt's fans and Gordon's fans mixed like oil and water, the two drivers shared great respect for each other. In many ways, they formed successive links in the great chain of progress that NASCAR has enjoyed through their success on the track and their ability to capitalize on that off the track.

Earnhardt helped revolutionize the NASCAR merchandising world and stood as the sport's most recognizable face for many years. Gordon came along and assumed some of that role, moving his popularity a little more uptown than Earnhardt's down-home appeal. As the sport tried to get more attention in places like New York and Los Angeles, Gordon was a better fit.

Since Gordon already has won more championships than anyone other than Earnhardt and Petty, and since he's already among the all-time leaders in almost every meaningful category, Gordon's place in the sport's history has already been the subject of considerable debate. For his part, Gordon says that someday when he's all done racing he will take the time to sit down and look back on what he's done and see how it stacks up.

"I never said I was going to win eight championships, or seven," said Gordon, who was engaged to be married again during the 2006 season. "I won the first championship and I was blown away. I won two championships and I was like, 'Holy cow, I can't believe this.'

"We work our butts off to try to win championships, but we never expect to. I'm not out to prove anything, to beat any statistics or records or anything like that. I've far exceeded anything that I ever dreamed I would have accomplished. Now it's just about giving my best every single week.

"I know what we're capable of. I do still think we have what it takes to win championships or I wouldn't be out here."—D.P.

His Own Dale

There was a time when Dale Earnhardt Jr. knew exactly what to do. Actually, it was all pretty simple. He'd merely figure out what he thought his father would like for him to do in a given situation. Then he would do the opposite.

It drove Dale Earnhardt nuts, for instance, that his son stayed up late, and it aggravated the elder Earnhardt even more that his son liked to stay in bed until sometime around noon. So every chance he got, Dale Jr. would talk about how late he stayed up and how late he got up. Earnhardt was an avid outdoorsman who talked in rhapsodic terms about how much he enjoyed going hunting. In one of the first major attention-gathering interviews he ever did, in *Rolling Stone* magazine, Earnhardt Jr. basically ridiculed the concept of hunting.

Perhaps it was a little bit of payback for the tough times, early in Earnhardt Jr.'s life when his father wasn't yet as famous and successful as he would wind up being and was forced to make some very difficult choices. Perhaps it was just a kid seeing how far his father would actually let him go.

"When my dad was here I could just about do whatever I wanted to and get away with it," Earnhardt Jr. once said. "I always had him to fall back on.... If I didn't do something right, it was his fault."

And then it all changed.

Before the 2001 Winston Cup season began, Earnhardt Jr. told reporters in a preseason news conference that he'd had a dream in which he won the Daytona 500 in just his second full season in the sport.

"I was out front all day," he said of the dream.

By the
NUMBERS

Dale versus Dale Jr.

Earnhardt	Races	Wins	Top 10s	Finish
1979	27	1	17	7th
1980	31	5	24	1st
1981	31	0	17	7th
1982	30	1	12	12th
1983	30	2	14	8th
1984	30	2	22	4th
Totals	182	11	106	

Earnhardt Jr.	Races	Wins	Top 10s	Finish
2000	34	2	5	16th
2001	36	3	15	8th
2002	36	2	16	11th
2003	36	2	21	3rd
2004	36	6	21	5th
2005	36	1	13	19th
Totals	210	16	91	

Source: www.racing-reference.info

The reporters knew they had the makings of a good story. Earnhardt would be running in that race, too, and if Earnhardt Jr. was out front and on his way to victory, where was his father in this dream?

"He wasn't there," Earnhardt Jr. said.

On February 18, 2001, Earnhardt Jr. was at the front of the pack as the sport's biggest race wound down. But Earnhardt Jr., who'd won two points races and the Winston all-star race in his rookie season in 2000, was not in first place. He was second, trailing only Michael Waltrip in another car owned by Dale Earnhardt Inc. to the checkered flag.

Behind those two cars, however, there was a big wreck. The elder Earnhardt had been running third, but coming out of Turn 3 his car got turned and he slid up the steep banking at Daytona into the outside wall. Almost at the same instant, Ken Schrader's car was running into the side of the black No. 3 Chevrolet.

TOP 10

Victory Leaders in NASCAR's Premier Series (2000–2005)

	Driver	Wins	Races	Top 5s	Poles	Earnings
1.	Jeff Gordon	25	214	81	24	$43,027,590
2.	Tony Stewart	21	214	81	8	$45,288,180
3.	Jimmie Johnson	18	147	53	8	$28,268,551
4.	Dale Earnhardt Jr.	16	214	59	6	$35,678,350
5.	Kurt Busch	14	184	43	3	$30,520,726
6.	Ryan Newman	12	152	52	35	$25,564,403
7.	Dale Jarrett	10	214	48	9	$30,341,283
8.	Matt Kenseth	10	214	50	3	$33,350,726
9.	Greg Biffle	9	114	22	1	$15,647,375
10.	Bobby Labonte	9	214	54	8	$31,885,802

Source: www.racing-reference.info

The combination of those two blows was more than even Earnhardt, who many considered something of a Superman for his legendary toughness, could endure.

The sport had lost one of the greatest champions it will ever know.

Dale Earnhardt Jr. had lost a father.

He also had lost a mentor, an advisor, and a feeling of security that came from knowing one of the great stand-up guys of all time had his back.

At the same time, he'd gained an army of fans who immediately swapped years of allegiance to his father onto the shoulders of a young man just trying to begin his career, as well as a large dose of the responsibility for making sure the company his father and step-mother, Teresa, had started did not fail or even falter.

"Before," said Ty Norris, a former executive for motorsports at DEI, "Dale Jr. didn't have to be the guy. Dale took care of the money side, the personnel side, he was dealing with the day-to-day issues and signing the checks. He was the guy who said, 'This is where you have to be, this is what time you have to be there, this is how you're going to get there, and this is where you're going to sit when you get there.'

"Dale Jr. didn't have to think; he didn't want to. He just wanted to go drive. And then he felt like it all fell on his shoulders immediately."

It was, of course, a difficult transition for the driver of the red No. 8 Chevrolets, whose colors dominate the grandstands at virtually every NASCAR track as fans show their continuing allegiance to the Earnhardt nation. Personally and professionally, life would never be the same.

But Earnhardt Jr. is, after all, an Earnhardt. Racing courses through his veins in a bloodline begun by his grandfather and carried to him by a father who made Earnhardt Jr., his brother, Kerry, and his sister, Kelley, work almost as hard for what they got as Ralph Earnhardt had made Dale Sr. work.

Earnhardt Jr. understands full well that it's his popularity and the performance of that No. 8 car that, going forward, will make or break the company. But he does have plenty of help and support to rely on.

First, of course, there is Teresa Earnhardt. Earnhardt's third wife and the mother of his fourth child, Taylor Nicole, Teresa took over the reins at DEI after her husband's death and continues to employ the same business and marketing savvy she used to help Earnhardt build it in the first place.

TRIVIA

As of the end of the 2005 season, who were the youngest and the oldest drivers ever to win the Nextel Cup championship?

Answers to the trivia questions are on pages 180–181.

The relationship between Earnhardt Jr. and his stepmother can best be described as complicated. They have not seen eye-to-eye about some business decisions since Earnhardt's death, but in reality the challenges run much further back.

Earnhardt Jr. was six and Kelley was eight when, in 1981, the house they were living in with their mother, Brenda, was badly damaged in a fire. Earnhardt had finally made it to NASCAR's big leagues, having won his first career championship the previous year,

TRIVIA

Which driver started the most races without scoring a Cup victory?

Answers to the trivia questions are on pages 180–181.

and it was decided that it would be better for everyone if the kids went to live with him. But during that season, Earnhardt's team was sold and he wound up looking for a new ride. He was also engaged to be married again, to Teresa.

"Dad was there when he could be," Kelley said. "But he was still making the kind of sacrifices he had to make to become what he wanted to be. Dale Jr. and I stayed with nannies or relatives.

"We didn't have that normal childhood, where the father comes home at five o'clock for dinner. It pretty much put Dale Jr. and me into survival mode. It has just always seemed to come down to Dale Jr. and me."

Kelley Earnhardt Elledge now serves as president of JR Motorsports, which fields a Busch Series team as well as cars in smaller racing divisions. Their mother, now Brenda Jackson, works there, too.

In 2006, Kelley and Teresa Earnhardt worked out a deal that gives Earnhardt Jr. rights to use his own name and signature in business ventures. Because he'd let his father make so many of the decisions for him, Earnhardt Jr. had never worried about things like that. After Earnhardt's death, Earnhardt Jr. signed those rights over to DEI to help make things work in the aftermath of the tragedy. But as he has matured, he has formed his own views of what he'd like to do in the sport. He and Kelley signed a deal last year to make a new racing complex in Alabama the first in a series of "Dale Earnhardt Jr. signature" facilities, for example.

Rumors continually swirl that Earnhardt Jr. might leave DEI to go drive for Richard Childress, who owned his father's cars. The No. 3 has not been used since Earnhardt's death, and many believe Earnhardt Jr. is the only driver who should be allowed to bring it back to the track. But Earnhardt Jr. has years of his own identity built up in the No. 8 car sponsored by Budweiser. He also cares intently about DEI and its legacy.

"Dale Jr. and I are very proud of what our dad did, and we want to continue to help DEI in reaching his vision for that company,"

Kelley said. "But we all have to work toward that with the same manner. Sometimes it just doesn't make a good team when you look at decisions from different ends of the spectrum. I don't think there's anything negative about the way we do business or the way Teresa does business. Sometimes we just look at it very differently."

What is likely the best thing for all parties, of course, would be for Earnhardt Jr. to keep the No. 8 car prominent in Nextel Cup competition. He went into the 2006 season with 16 career victories, including emotional Daytona victories in July 2001 in the first race there after his father's death and in the 2004 Daytona 500. After missing the Chase for the Nextel Cup in 2005, he battled his way back into that 10-race championship playoff in 2006 aided by his 17th career win at Richmond in May.

After a disappointing 19th-place finish in the standings in 2005, Dale Earnhardt Jr. qualified for the Chase for the Nextel Cup in 2006. Photo courtesy of David Durochik/SportPics.

Earnhardt Jr. is 32 years old. After a difficult 2005, in which he finished 19th in points after an ill-fated decision to change crew chiefs before that season began, he and his cousin Tony Eury Jr. were reunited. Eury Jr. assisted his father, Tony Sr., on Earnhardt Jr.'s team before the switch, and in late 2005 Eury Jr. returned to take over as crew chief on the No. 8. He and Earnhardt Jr. both say they've matured, and their ability to make the Chase in 2006 shows they're moving in the right direction.

There is one more critical factor in the equation as Earnhardt Jr. tries to move forward and ultimately fulfill his promise as not only a winner but, someday, a champion in the sport. Even though Dale Sr. is no longer around to fall back on—or to annoy—he's still a big part of his son's life.

"The majority of my enjoyment was seeing how proud my father was and to see how happy he was after I won," Earnhardt said. "That's not there anymore. But I got a lot of advice from my father and I probably rely on that now more than ever."—D.P.

Discovering Columbus

Along the way from the Dairy Queen near downtown Columbus, Indiana, to the house where Tony Stewart grew up, you make a left onto Home Avenue.

Home is more than an address to Stewart, though. When he moved back there after the 2004 season, right into that same house where he lived when Bob Franke, the owner of that Dairy Queen, became the first person to sponsor Stewart's racing career, Stewart seemed to reconnect with an important part of who he was.

"The people in Columbus...realize I do what I do on the weekends," Stewart said. "That's my job. But at home, I'm just another one of the guys."

In more ways than you might think possible, that's the way things are in the small town less than an hour's drive from Indianapolis Motor Speedway. Stewart eats in locally owned restaurants and plays cards with the guys at a local civic club. He rides around town, sometimes on a motorcycle and sometimes in the hearse he's had tricked out, and his neighbors wave.

They know, of course, that Stewart might very well be the most versatile race-car driver alive today. They know that the Nextel Cup championship he won in 2005 gives him two NASCAR championships in his career, making him one of only 14 men to have ever won more than one title in stock-car racing's top series. They know he's also won a championship in the Indy Racing League, and many of them hope one day he'll come back to the open-wheel side of the sport and try once again to win the Indianapolis 500.

The people of Columbus also know that Stewart has bought a large estate on the outskirts of town, where someday he'll move into a large mansion and spend as much time as he possibly can fishing in the lake on his property that he had drained, reworked, and stocked. They also know that when he's in Columbus Stewart would much rather talk about what's biting than about his No. 20 Chevrolet race car. And they're okay with that.

The house where it all began is in a middle-class neighborhood. When the band at the high school Stewart attended tuned up for its football halftime shows, you could sit on the front porch and tap your toe to the beat.

Many consider Tony Stewart the most versatile race car driver alive today.
Photo courtesy of David Durochik/SportPics.

Stewart says he was the kid "who used to play in the backyard and smack a baseball into the aluminum siding of the neighbors' houses and they'd be coming out screaming." He also had a go-kart, one that he and his father, Nelson, worked on together. Nelson Stewart wanted his son to have fun, but he also wanted Tony to know that anything worth doing was worth doing well. That lesson came on one of their first trips to a track.

"He was running around playing somewhere and I needed him for something and I couldn't find him," Nelson said. "I found him and I sat him down and said, 'If you want to play, we'll stay home and you can play in the yard. If we're going to make the effort to come to the track, though, we're going to be serious about it.'"

Stewart got serious about racing, all right. After winning championships in his go-kart while still a lad, he moved up to the U.S. Auto Club's sprint- and midget-car ranks and was the national midget series champion at age 20. The next year, in 1995, he won USAC's midget, sprint, and Silver Crown series national titles in the same year.

Stewart remembers the exact moment he decided that he was a race-car driver.

"I was working at a machine shop for $5 an hour in the middle of the country in Rush County, Indiana," Stewart said. "I sat in a big barn on a metal stool on a concrete floor at a drill press and was picking up parts out of a five-gallon bucket full of solvent."

That winter, he went to Phoenix to race a Silver Crown car in the Copper Classic.

"I ran second to Mike Bliss out there," Stewart said. "My portion of the prize money was like $3,500. When I came back to work on Monday, I was sitting at that drill press and started trying to figure out how many $5 hours I had to work to make $3,500. I thought, 'When I drive race cars I can get up at noon, I'm at the pit gate by 4:00, I'm done at midnight, and I'm still wide awake. If I can do that three nights a week and pay my bills I don't have to get up at 7:30 and drive to work and work five days a week. I was too lazy to work a real job. That's the God's honest truth."

He won his IRL title in 1997, but he was already looking hard at NASCAR at that time. When he first met with team owner Joe Gibbs, who would eventually put Stewart in the No. 20 cars he is still making famous, it was Stewart who asked to run a full year in the Busch Series before stepping up.

"It said to me he was more interested in being well prepared for what he was going into," Gibbs said. "He wanted to win at it and he wanted to make sure—he told me this—that he didn't do something stupid in front of his peers."

That has never happened, at least not in terms of how well Stewart has competed. But there have been times when something his father once said has particular relevance.

"He's just so intense at the track," Nelson Stewart said, "it's like he's a totally different person."

When he was racing Indy cars, Stewart's nickname was "Tony the Temper," and his NASCAR career has been pocked by several incidents in which Stewart let his emotions get the best of him. But he is also trying to learn to pick his battles. He doesn't always succeed, but on his way to the 2005 championship he seemed more poised and more content than ever before.

"You get tired of being uptight about everything all the time," Stewart said. "I could be right about a topic, but it's just not even worth fighting sometimes. It's just easier to go through the motions instead of having to stand up for what you think is right on a particular day and then having to defend yourself the next two or three days. That's part of it—just learning what fights are really worth fighting and which ones aren't."

When the 2006 season opened at Daytona, Stewart felt that drivers were getting too aggressive with "bump drafting," the practice of bumping a car in front of yours to give it a big push of momentum. He spoke out, warning that someone could get hurt or killed if NASCAR didn't act. NASCAR did, first enforcing "no bump" zones and later enacting new rules regarding the beefed-up bumpers the cars were using in races where drafting is practiced.

"My attitude was, 'Hey, this is something that's on my mind,'"

TRIVIA

Two drivers have won both the Indianapolis 500 and the Daytona 500 in their careers. Can you name them?

Answers to the trivia questions are on pages 180–181.

THREE
OF A KIND

Seventeen drivers have won at least one race in the Nextel Cup, Busch, and Craftsman Truck series in their careers, and 17 also have won poles in all three series.

Wins in each series	Poles in each series
Johnny Benson	Johnny Benson
Greg Biffle	Greg Biffle
Kurt Busch	Geoffrey Bodine
Kyle Busch	Todd Bodine
Ricky Craven	Chuck Bown
Carl Edwards	Kyle Busch
Bobby Hamilton	Stacy Compton
Kevin Harvick	Carl Edwards
Kasey Kahne	Terry Labonte
Bobby Labonte	Jason Leffler
Terry Labonte	Mark Martin
Mark Martin	Jamie McMurray
Jamie McMurray	Scott Riggs
Steve Park	Boris Said
Ken Schrader	Ken Schrader
Jimmy Spencer	Mike Skinner
Tony Stewart	Jimmy Spencer

Stewart said following his meeting with NASCAR officials after making his comments. "I told them, 'I want to tell you what went on out there in my opinion and from my perspective, and what you do with it from there is up to you guys.'

"[But] I won't be that vocal in the media about a topic again.... I tried to do something to help and all it has done is create extra work.... And it shouldn't have to be that way.

"You don't get an instructional video. They don't give you a freshman pamphlet saying: 'This is what your life is going to be like. This is how you do things. This is what is going to happen to you when you're in the garage area.' None of that is explained to you. It is trial and error, and Lord knows I've had enough trials and errors, and more errors than trials. But as you go on, you learn. You learn about how to deal with the things."

When he won his first championship in 2002, Stewart said the best thing about being a NASCAR Cup Series champion was that it gave him something to hold over his hero's head.

"I finally did something A.J. Foyt didn't do," Stewart said. "The first Indy car I ever drove was for A.J. at Phoenix. It was one of the most frustrating experiences of my life. But it was one of the best experiences of my life, too. The relationship I built with A.J. that week will last a lifetime. I never got verbally beat up as bad with anybody as I did with A.J. for five days. When I was proud of something I did, he would say, 'Just check the record books, big boy.' That was his favorite quote: 'Just check the record books.'

TRIVIA

Since 1972, no driver has won more than four consecutive Nextel Cup races. Seven different drivers share that modern-era record. Name them.

Answers to the trivia questions are on pages 180–181.

"Well, A.J.—check the record book! He may have won Daytona and he may have won Indy, but he hasn't won an Indy car championship and a stock-car championship. I finally got one up on the old man."

Stewart is proud of the versatility he's shown in racing. By his own count, he's won races in 21 different series. He's tried 22, but so far he hasn't won the Rolex 24-hour race at Daytona. You can bet he will keep on trying until he does.

In NASCAR, he won his 26th Cup race at Daytona in July of 2006. But he barely missed qualifying for the Chase for the Nextel Cup, denying him the chance to try to repeat as champion.

Among those career victories, none will likely ever be more special than his victory in the Allstate 400 at the Brickyard in 2005. Stewart lived around and worked in Indianapolis his whole life, and he went to the Indianapolis 500 for the first time when he was five years old. He had cars that seemed fast enough to win that race several times before coming to NASCAR, and twice he has run in the

Indy 500 on the same day as the Coca-Cola 600 at Lowe's Motor Speedway at Charlotte since making that move.

In August 2005, though, he finally got that victory at Indy. As the laps wound down, Stewart said he could see his father standing outside of Turn 2 trying to coach Tony home to that emotional victory.

That night, it was banana splits for everybody at the Dairy Queen in Columbus.—D.P.

Who's Next?

Men like Lee Petty, Buck Baker, Richard Petty, David Pearson, Bobby Allison, Cale Yarborough, and Dale Earnhardt, some of the legends who've been covered in this book, are all members of more halls of fame than you can shake a tire iron at.

The National Motorsports Press Association has its Stock Car Racing Hall of Fame as part of the museum at Darlington Raceway in South Carolina. The International Motorsports Hall of Fame, located adjacent to Talladega Superspeedway in Alabama, has a large stock-car contingent among its broader group of racing heroes.

NASCAR has never had its own officially sanctioned hall of fame and historical museum, but that's about to change. In early 2006, NASCAR announced that it had chosen Charlotte, North Carolina, as the site of what's promised to be a high-tech, state-of-the-art shrine to a sport that has worked very hard to keep technology as far out of the equation as possible so as to allow the drivers and the crews who work on the cars to truly make the difference between success and failure.

Groundbreaking for the new museum is scheduled to take place in early 2007, and the schedule calls for it to open no later than 2010. Before opening day, there will surely be endless arguments about who should be part of the first few classes of inductees, but eventually all of the sport's greatest will be there.

Meanwhile, out there on racetracks all across America, another generation of drivers will be banging fenders and rubbing paint as they try to write their own résumés and dream of one day being remembered by their fans the way longtime followers of the sport remember the Curtis Turners, the Tim Flocks, the Ned Jarretts, and

By the NUMBERS The average age of a NASCAR race winner, all time, is 34.2 years. It's higher, at 35.5 years, in the so-called modern era, since 1972, but the trend is reversing. The 2003, 2004, and 2005 seasons were among the 10 seasons with the youngest average age of a winner, and through the first 27 races of 2006 the number was down even more. Here are the 10 seasons with the lowest and highest average winner's ages.

Lowest average winner's age		Highest average winner's age	
Year	Avg. age	Year	Avg. age
1950	28.59	1983	38.90
1951	29.44	1982	38.62
2006	30.39	1991	38.38
1952	30.67	1978	38.17
1967	31.22	1976	38.15
1963	31.43	1981	37.99
2004	31.45	1994	37.85
2005	31.71	1993	37.75
2003	31.74	1984	37.71
1964	31.75	1979	37.68

the Tim Richmonds. And judging from the array of talent on display in the NASCAR Nextel Cup Series these days, NASCAR and Charlotte had better leave some room to grow in that new hall of fame they're planning.

One of the great truisms in sport is that every generation believes the athletes they grew up watching are the greatest ever. Try to convince a baseball fan who grew up watching Mickey Mantle, Ted Williams, and Stan Musial that today's hitters are better. In the mind of a San Francisco 49ers fan from the glory days, Joe Montana never threw an interception, fumbled a snap, or missed an open receiver. Pro basketball fans who saw Julius Erving and David Thompson play in the old American Basketball Association will swear they saw them take off at the free-throw line and make a dunk, and argue you down they could have done it from the top of the key if they wanted to.

By the
NUMBERS
A look at what percentage of races were won by drivers in the following starting spots at the tracks currently on the Nextel Cup circuit (through August 31, 2006):

Position	1999–2006	1949–1998	All-time
Pole	12.3%	18.5%	17.1%
Top five	41.4%	62.3%	57.5%
Top 10	57.5%	82.5%	76.6%
Top 20	82.4%	96.7%	93.4%
26th-plus	11.1%	1.1%	3.4%

Sources: 2006 NASCAR Media Guide and NASCAR Statistical Services

Race fans are no different. The sport is never greater than it used to be. You can show them old records that prove that the winners of many races in the 1960s finished several laps ahead of the next car, but in their memories every Sunday cars were coming under the checkered flag three or four wide with at least one of them upside down and on fire.

Reality, of course, is this: In every race season, there are great finishes and there are routs. There are days when one driver and his team show up with a superior car and have everybody else covered, and then there are days when cars swap the lead as fast and as often as 14-year-old girls change boyfriends.

This, also, is true of sport. At whatever point in history you're standing, it seems that things have never been as big, as fast, as exciting, or as competitive as they are now.

But hey, come on. Take a look.

In 2003, 2004, and 2005, 52 of 108 races were won by drivers who hadn't yet reached their 30th birthdays. In NASCAR history, only about 23.5 percent of all races have been won by drivers that age or younger, but in those three seasons that rate almost exactly doubled.

What's going on?

Well, in 2004 when 20 of 36 race winners were not yet 30, drivers like Jimmie Johnson, Kurt Busch, Elliott Sadler, Dale Earnhardt Jr., and Ryan Newman were all with top-tier teams and had top-flight equipment. In 2005, Kasey Kahne, Carl Edwards, and Kyle Busch—

who at just over 20 years and four months old became the youngest Cup race winner ever at California Speedway—joined the fun. Then in 2006, Denny Hamlin became the sport's latest next big thing.

Given that those drivers are only slightly younger than Jeff Gordon, Tony Stewart, and Matt Kenseth—all of whom, along with Kurt Busch, have won championships—it certainly seems that talent is a renewable resource in stock-car racing.

Unquestionably, things have changed dramatically in the sport in the past decade. Formerly the pattern was for a driver to get in a car for the first time perhaps as a teenager or soon thereafter. After a few years of slinging cars around local short tracks, the best moved up to regional series and a few of the very best found a place to serve tours as apprentices in mediocre to poor equipment in the big leagues. Only then, after showing their mettle and their determination, did the lucky ones get a shot in one of the handful of truly good rides there were in the sport.

Jimmie Johnson is just one of a large group of young drivers striving to become the sport's next superstar. Photo courtesy of David Durochik/SportPics.

In the modern NASCAR world, one car owner recently said that the best résumé a driver can have is a blank one. Manufacturers and multicar teams, looking for the next Jeff Gordon or Kyle Busch, have signed up teenagers who've been racing since they were old enough to get off a tricycle and placed them in aggressive driver development programs aimed at moving them to the Nextel Cup as rapidly as possible.

Reed Sorenson, who ran a full season as Cup rookie in 2006, was born in February 1986. He was six years old when Jeff Gordon, who's still no codger in his own right, made his Cup debut!

Without question, there's already a spot reserved for Gordon in that new hall of fame being built in Charlotte, the city where that historic first race happened in 1949. Before they're done, Stewart or Johnson or some of the other stars fueling the sport's popularity today will be there, too. As it has from inaugural champion Red Byron right on down the line, the sport's torch will pass through their hands to the next generation and to the next.

That is, of course, if the men who lead the sport continue to do their jobs the way they have to bring NASCAR from where it was to where it is today.

The 2007 Nextel Cup season is one major change to the sport. Toyota is fielding teams in the sport's top series, the first foreign nameplate to do that full time in the sport's history. In 16 of the 36 races held in NASCAR's 59th season, teams are scheduled to race in new cars designed to be safer and to increase the level and fairness of competition. By 2009, those cars are scheduled to be used in all races, and the outcome of success of this "car of tomorrow" project has huge long-term ramifications for the sport. A new television deal goes into effect, returning portions of the Cup schedule and the entire Busch Series schedule to former partner ABC/ESPN while continuing relationships with Fox, TNT, and Speed.

Think how difficult it would have been for the men who gathered in the Streamline Hotel in Daytona Beach, Florida, in December 1947 to have closed their eyes and imagined what they were starting would look like today. Even in their wildest imaginations, could any of them have seen a 2.5-mile paved speedway, built just a few miles inland from where they sat, becoming a world-renowned center for

By the NUMBERS

NASCAR Cup victories broken down by the age of the winner (includes races through September 17, 2006):

Age	Wins	Percent
Before 25	46	2.2%
25–29	451	21.3%
30–34	771	36.4%
35–39	531	25.1%
40–44	240	11.3%
45–49	69	3.3%
50-plus	10	0.5%

Youngest race winner—Kyle Busch (20 years, four months, two days)

Oldest race winner—Harry Gant (52 years, seven months, six days)

all manners of racing? Could they have imagined stock cars racing at Indianapolis? Could they have even dreamed of a place like Bristol Motor Speedway, where nearly 175,000 fans pack themselves around a half-mile oval and hang on every bump and every grind?

At the same time, it's almost as difficult right now to close your eyes and allow yourself to imagine stock-car racing growing as much in the next 10 years as it has in the previous 10, but that has to be the goal. Remember what Bill France Jr. said in the second chapter of this book? "We've just got to keep pushing the race cars up the hill. We have to keep the sport moving forward."

On the day France said that, a reporter came back with a follow-up question. What would it be like, France was asked, if NASCAR ever got all the way up that hill?

"I don't want to get to the top," he said. "We want to get as close to it as we can. I want to be able to see over it. But the hill needs to get higher and higher as we go up the road." —D.P.

ANSWERS TO TRIVIA QUESTIONS

Page 10: The victory was awarded to Bill France Sr. In addition to promoting the race, France also drove in it and finished second. Although he credited himself with the victory after disqualifying the winner, he gave the winner's share of the purse to the driver who finished third.

Page 21: Flock's win on August 12, 1956, was particularly special because the track was only 25 miles from Fon du Lac, Wisconsin, the home office of Mercury Outboard Motors. Flock had left the Mercury Outboard team owned by Carl Kiekhaefer that April under bad terms. "This was one he [Kiekhaefer] wanted badly, and I won it," Flock said.

Page 23: Buck Baker was originally scored the race winner of the 1963 Turkey Day 200, but Wendell Scott protested that ruling and eventually was awarded the victory. It would be the only career victory in 495 career starts for Scott, who is the only African American to win a race at the sport's top level.

Page 35: The first night race at a superspeedway was held in 1955, at a one-mile dirt track in Raleigh, North Carolina.

Page 35: The 12 states that have not hosted a race are Vermont, Rhode Island, Idaho, Montana, Wyoming, Minnesota, North Dakota, New Mexico, Colorado, Utah, Mississippi, and Missouri. (Remember, Kansas Speedway is in Kansas.)

Page 86: One driver topped the $1 million mark in career earnings from 1949 through 1971: Richard Petty, with just over $1.3 million. David Pearson was second with $788,596.

Page 88: The race Bobby Isaac won at Greenville-Pickens Speedway in April 1971 was the first race televised live from start to finish on network TV, with Jim McKay anchoring the broadcast on ABC's *Wide World of Sports.*

Page 90: Bobby Isaac holds the record for most poles in a season with 20 poles in 1969.

Page 90: Cale Yarborough twice won on his birthday.

Page 102: Richard Petty (52,194 laps led), Cale Yarborough (31,677), Bobby Allison (27,539), Dale Earnhardt (25,707), David Pearson (25,424), and Darrell Waltrip (23,131) are the only six drivers to have led more than 20,000 laps in their Cup careers.

Page 134: The No. 11, with 180 victories, is second on the list.

Page 137: Lorenzen's car owner was Mamie Reynolds, the first woman to be the official owner of a race-winner in NASCAR's top series.

Page 163: The youngest champion was 1950 winner Bill Rexford, who was 23 years, eight months, and 17 days old as of November 15 of that year. The oldest was Bobby Allison, who was 45 years, 11 months, and 28 days old as of November 15, 1983.

Page 164: J.D. McDuffie, winless in 653 tries, has started the most races without scoring a Cup victory.

Page 170: Mario Andretti and A.J. Foyt won both the Indianapolis 500 and the Daytona 500.

Page 172: Cale Yarborough (in 1976), Darrell Waltrip (1981), Dale Earnhardt (1987), Harry Gant (1991), Bill Elliott (1992), Mark Martin (1993), and Jeff Gordon (1988) have each won more than four consecutive Nextel Cup races.

Appendix A:
NASCAR Tracks

The following is a list of tracks where NASCAR's top series (now called the Nextel Cup) have run races, listed by state and then chronologically by date of the first race held at that track.

Date of first race	Track name	Location
Alabama		
4/8/1951	Lakeview Speedway	Mobile
4/17/1955	Montgomery Motor Speedway	Montgomery
9/9/1956	Chisholm Speedway	Montgomery
9/7/1958	Birmingham Fairgrounds	Birmingham
8/3/1960	Dixie Speedway	Birmingham
8/8/1962	Huntsville Speedway	Huntsville
9/14/1969	Talladega Superspeedway	Talladega
Arizona		
4/22/1951	Arizona State Fairgrounds	Phoenix
5/15/1955	Tucson Rodeo Grounds	Tucson
11/6/1988	Phoenix International Raceway	Avondale
Arkansas		
10/10/1954	Memphis-Arkansas Speedway	LeHi
California		
4/8/1951	Carrell Speedway	Gardena
10/14/1951	Oakland Stadium	Oakland

10/28/1951	Marchbanks Speedway	Hanford
8/22/1954	Bay Meadows Race Track	San Mateo
11/20/1955	Willow Springs International Raceway	Lancaster
5/30/1956	Redwood Speedway	Eureka
6/3/1956	Merced Fairgrounds	Merced
7/8/1956	California State Fairgrounds	Sacramento
6/8/1957	Ascot Stadium	Los Angeles
6/22/1957	Capital Speedway	Sacramento
9/15/1957	Santa Clara Fairgrounds	San Jose
6/1/1958	Riverside International Raceway	Riverside
2/28/1971	Ontario Motor Speedway	Ontario
6/11/1989	Infineon Raceway	Sonoma
6/22/1997	California Speedway	Fontana

Connecticut
10/12/1951	Thompson International Speedway	Thompson

Delaware
7/6/1969	Dover International Speedway	Dover

Florida
7/10/1949	Daytona beach course	Daytona Beach
11/4/1951	Jacksonville Speedway Park	Jacksonville
1/20/1952	Palm Beach Speedway	West Palm Beach
6/14/1953	Five Flags Speedway	Pensacola
12/30/1956	Titusville-Cocoa Speedway	Titusville
2/20/1959	Daytona International Speedway	Daytona Beach
11/11/1962	Golden Gate Speedway	Tampa
11/14/1999	Homestead-Miami Speedway	Homestead

Georgia
6/10/1951	Columbus Speedway	Columbus
9/8/1951	Central City Speedway	Macon
11/11/1951	Lakewood Speedway	Atlanta
6/1/1952	Hayloft Speedway	Augusta
3/28/1954	Oglethorpe Speedway	Savannah

7/31/1960	Atlanta Motor Speedway	Hampton
3/17/1962	Savannah Speedway	Savannah
6/19/1962	Augusta International Speedway	Augusta
8/25/1962	Valdosta 75 Speedway	Valdosta
11/17/1963	Augusta Raceway (road)	Augusta
5/10/1966	Middle Georgia Raceway	Macon
11/3/1968	Jeffco Speedway	Jefferson

Illinois
7/10/1954	Santa Fe Speedway	Willow Springs
7/21/1956	Soldier Field	Chicago
7/15/2001	Chicagoland Speedway	Joliet

Indiana
10/15/1950	Winchester Speedway	Winchester
7/20/1952	Playland Park Speedway	South Bend
8/6/1994	Indianapolis Motor Speedway	Indianapolis

Iowa
| 8/2/1953 | Davenport Speedway | Davenport |

Kansas
| 9/30/2001 | Kansas Speedway | Kansas City |

Kentucky
| 8/29/1954 | Corbin Speedway | Corbin |

Louisiana
| 6/7/1953 | Louisiana Fairgrounds | Shreveport |

Maine
| 7/12/1966 | Oxford Plains Speedway | Oxford |

Maryland
| 8/25/1965 | Beltsville Speedway | Beltsville |

Massachusetts
6/17/1961	Norwood Arena	Norwood

Michigan
7/1/1951	Grand River Speedrome	Grand Rapids
8/12/1951	Michigan State Fairgrounds	Detroit
7/6/1952	Monroe Speedway	Monroe
6/15/1969	Michigan International Speedway	Brooklyn

Nebraska
7/26/1953	Lincoln County Fairgrounds	North Platte

Nevada
10/16/1955	Las Vegas Park Speedway	Las Vegas
3/1/1998	Las Vegas Motor Speedway	Las Vegas

New Hampshire
7/11/1993	New Hampshire International Speedway	Loudon

New Jersey
8/24/1951	Morristown Speedway	Morristown
6/13/1954	Linden Airport	Linden
7/26/1958	Wall Stadium	Belmar
8/17/1956	Old Bridge Stadium	Old Bridge
5/30/1958	Trenton Speedway	Trenton

New York
9/18/1949	Hamburg Speedway	Hamburg
6/18/1950	Vernon Fairgrounds	Vernon
7/2/1950	Monroe County Fairgrounds	Rochester
8/1/1951	Altamont Fairgrounds	Altamont
7/4/1952	Shangri-La Speedway	Oswego
6/18/1955	Fonda Speedway	Fonda
6/19/1955	Airborne Speedway	Plattsburg
7/30/1955	New York State Fairgrounds	Syracuse
8/4/1957	Watkins Glen International	Watkins Glen

7/16/1958	State Line Speedway	Busti
7/19/1958	Buffalo Civic Stadium	Buffalo
8/3/1958	Bridgehampton (road)	Bridgehampton
7/17/1960	Montgomery Air Base	Montgomery
7/15/1964	Islip Speedway	Islip
7/7/1970	Albany-Saratoga Speedway	Malta

North Carolina

6/19/1949	Charlotte Speedway	Charlotte
8/7/1949	Occoneechee Speedway	Hillsboro
10/16/1949	North Wilkesboro Speedway	North Wilkesboro
7/29/1951	Asheville-Weaverville Speedway	Weaverville
9/30/1951	Wilson Speedway	Wilson
3/8/1953	Harnett Speedway	Spring Lake
5/9/1953	Hickory Motor Speedway	Hickory
5/30/1953	Raleigh Speedway	Raleigh
6/23/1953	Tri-City Speedway	High Point
8/13/1954	Southern States Fairgrounds	Charlotte
5/28/1955	N.C. State Fairgrounds	Raleigh
5/29/1955	Forsyth County Fairgrounds	Winston-Salem
5/6/1956	Concord Speedway	Concord
7/17/1956	Cleveland County Fairgrounds	Shelby
4/28/1957	Greensboro Fairgrounds	Greensboro
6/30/1957	Jacksonville Speedway	Jacksonville
11/3/1957	Champion Speedway	Fayetteville
5/24/1958	Bowman Gray Stadium	Winston-Salem
7/12/1958	McCormick Field	Asheville
9/12/1958	Gastonia Fairgrounds	Gastonia
10/5/1958	Salisbury Superspeedway	Salisbury
6/19/1960	Lowe's Motor Speedway	Charlotte
7/13/1962	Asheville Speedway	Asheville
9/11/1962	Dog Track Speedway	Moyock
11/22/1962	Tar Heel Speedway	Randleman
10/25/1964	Harris Speedway	Harris
10/31/1965	North Carolina Speedway	Rockingham
5/13/1966	Starlite Speedway	Monroe

Ohio
5/30/1950	Canfield Fairgrounds	Canfield
6/25/1950	Dayton Speedway	Dayton
7/8/1951	Bainbridge Fairgrounds	Bainbridge
8/19/1951	Fort Miami Speedway	Toledo
5/24/1953	Powell Motor Speedway	Columbus

Oklahoma
| 8/3/1956 | Oklahoma State Fairgrounds | Oklahoma City |

Oregon
| 5/27/1956 | Portland Speedway | Portland |

Pennsylvania
9/11/1949	Langhorne Speedway	Langhorne
10/2/1949	Heidelberg Raceway	Pittsburgh
10/14/1951	Pine Grove Speedway	Shippensville
5/23/1954	Sharon Speedway	Sharon
6/27/1954	Williams Grove Speedway	Mechanicsburg
6/10/1955	Lincoln Speedway	New Oxford
6/12/1958	New Bradford Speedway	Bradford
6/15/1958	Reading Fairgrounds	Reading
8/4/1974	Pocono International Raceway	Long Pond

South Carolina
9/4/1950	Darlington Raceway	Darlington
6/16/1951	Columbia Speedway	Columbia
8/25/1951	Greenville-Pickens Speedway	Greenville
7/4/1953	Piedmont Interstate Fairgrounds	Spartanburg
8/25/1956	Coastal Speedway	Myrtle Beach
6/1/1957	Lancaster Speedway	Lancaster
10/12/1957	Newberry Speedway	Newberry
8/23/1958	Myrtle Beach Speedway	Myrtle Beach
9/15/1960	Gamecock Speedway	Sumter
6/23/1961	Hartsville Speedway	Hartsville

South Dakota
7/22/1953	Rapid Valley Speedway	Rapid City

Tennessee
10/7/1956	Tennessee-Carolina Speedway	Newport
8/10/1958	Nashville Fairgrounds Speedway	Nashville
7/29/1961	Bristol Motor Speedway	Bristol
8/3/1962	Boyd Speedway	Chattanooga
8/13/1965	Smoky Mountain Raceway	Maryville
6/19/1969	Kingsport Speedway	Kingsport

Texas
12/7/1969	Texas World Speedway	College Station
6/23/1971	Meyer Speedway	Houston
4/6/1997	Texas Motor Speedway	Fort Worth

Virginia
9/25/1949	Martinsville Speedway	Martinsville
4/19/1953	Richmond International Raceway	Richmond
8/23/1953	Princess Anne Speedway	Norfolk
8/22/1956	Norfolk Speedway	Norfolk
4/25/1958	Old Dominion Speedway	Manassas
5/15/1958	Starkey Speedway	Roanoke
8/20/1960	South Boston Speedway	South Boston
8/18/1961	Southside Speedway	Richmond
5/15/1964	Langley Field Speedway	Hampton

Washington
8/4/1957	Bremerton Raceway	Bremerton

West Virginia
8/18/1963	West Virginia International Speedway	Huntington

Wisconsin
8/12/1956	Road America	Elkhart Lake

Appendix A: NASCAR Tracks

Canada

| 7/1/1952 | Stamford Park | Niagara Falls, Ontario |
| 7/18/1958 | Canadian National Exposition Speedway | Toronto, Ontario |

Appendix B: All-Time NASCAR Cup Champions

Year	No.	Driver	Car Owner	Car Make	Winnings
1949	22	Red Byron	Raymond Parks	Oldsmobile	$5,800
1950	60	Bill Rexford	Julian Buesink	Oldsmobile	$6,175
1951	92	Herb Thomas	Herb Thomas	Hudson	$18,200
1952	91	Tim Flock	Ted Chester	Hudson	$20,210
1953	92	Herb Thomas	Herb Thomas	Hudson	$27,300
1954	42	Lee Petty	Petty Enterprises	Chrysler	$26,706
1955	300	Tim Flock	Carl Kiekhaefer	Chrysler	$33,705
1956	300	Buck Baker	Carl Kiekhaefer	Chrysler	$29,790
1957	87	Buck Baker	Buck Baker	Chevrolet	$24,712
1958	42	Lee Petty	Petty Enterprises	Oldsmobile	$20,600
1959	42	Lee Petty	Petty Enterprises	Plymouth	$45,570
1960	4	Rex White	Rex White	Chevrolet	$45,260
1961	11	Ned Jarrett	W.G. Holloway Jr.	Chevrolet	$27,285
1962	8	Joe Weatherly	Bud Moore	Pontiac	$56,110
1963	8	Joe Weatherly	Various	Mercury	$58,110
1964	43	Richard Petty	Petty Enterprises	Plymouth	$98,810
1965	11	Ned Jarrett	Bondy Long	Ford	$77,996
1966	6	David Pearson	Cotton Owens	Dodge	$59,205
1967	43	Richard Petty	Petty Enterprise	Plymouth	$130,275
1968	17	David Pearson	Holman-Moody	Ford	$118,842
1969	17	David Pearson	Holman-Moody	Ford	$183,700
1970	71	Bobby Isaac	Nord Krauskopf	Dodge	$121,470
1971	43	Richard Petty	Petty Enterprises	Plymouth	$309,225
1972	43	Richard Petty	Petty Enterprises	Plymouth	$227,015
1973	72	Benny Parsons	L.G. DeWitt	Chevrolet	$114,345
1974	43	Richard Petty	Petty Enterprises	Dodge	$299,175
1975	43	Richard Petty	Petty Enterprises	Dodge	$378,865
1976	11	Cale Yarborough	Junior Johnson	Chevrolet	$387,183
1977	11	Cale Yarborough	Junior Johnson	Chevrolet	$477,499
1978	11	Cale Yarborough	Junior Johnson	Chevrolet	$530,751
1979	43	Richard Petty	Petty Enterprises	Chevrolet	$531,292
1980	2	Dale Earnhardt	Rod Osterlund	Chevrolet	$588,926
1981	11	Darrell Waltrip	Junior Johnson	Chevrolet	$693,342

Appendix B: All-Time NASCAR Cup Champions

Year	No.	Driver	Car Owner	Car Make	Winnings
1982	11	Darrel Waltrip	Junior Johnson	Buick	$873,118
1983	22	Bobby Allison	Bill Gardner	Buick	$828,335
1984	44	Terry Labonte	Billy Hagan	Chevrolet	$713,010
1985	11	Darrell Waltrip	Junior Johnson	Chevrolet	$1,318,735
1986	3	Dale Earnhardt	Richard Childress	Chevrolet	$1,783,880
1987	3	Dale Earnhardt	Richard Childress	Chevrolet	$2,099,243
1988	9	Bill Elliott	Harry Melling	Ford	$1,574,639
1989	27	Rusty Wallace	Raymond Beadle	Pontiac	$2,247,950
1990	3	Dale Earnhardt	Richard Childress	Chevrolet	$3,083,056
1991	3	Dale Earnhardt	Richard Childress	Chevrolet	$2,416,685
1992	7	Alan Kulwicki	Alan Kulwicki	Ford	$2,322,561
1993	3	Dale Earnhardt	Richard Childress	Chevrolet	$3,353,789
1994	3	Dale Earnhardt	Richard Childress	Chevrolet	$3,300,733
1995	24	Jeff Gordon	Rick Hendrick	Chevrolet	$4,347,343
1996	5	Terry Labonte	Rick Hendrick	Chevrolet	$3,991,348
1997	24	Jeff Gordon	Rick Hendrick	Chevrolet	$6,375,658
1998	24	Jeff Gordon	Rick Hendrick	Chevrolet	$9,306,584
1999	88	Dale Jarrett	Robert Yates	Ford	$6,649,596
2000	18	Bobby Labonte	Joe Gibbs	Pontiac	$7,361,386
2001	24	Jeff Gordon	Rick Hendrick	Chevrolet	$10,879,757
2002	20	Tony Stewart	Joe Gibbs	Chevrolet	$9,163,761
2003	17	Matt Kenseth	Jack Roush	Ford	$9,422,764
2004	97	Kurt Busch	Jack Roush	Ford	$9,661,513
2005	20	Tony Stewart	Joe Gibbs	Chevrolet	$13,578,168

Source: NASCAR Statistical Services

NASCAR ESSENTIAL

All-Time Nextel Cup Driver List

Listed drivers have competed in at least 10 races or won at least one race in what is now the NASCAR Nextel Cup Series. List includes the driver's name, racing hometown, years competing, and total career starts as of September 22, 2006. Drivers in bold won at least one race, with the victory total in parentheses next to the name.

A

Marv Acton	Porterville, Calif.	1971, 1974, 1977	14
Carl Adams	National City, Calif.	1972–75	28
Weldon Adams	Augusta, Ga.	1950–53, 1962, 1964	25
Grant Adcox	Chattanooga, Tenn.	1974–79, 1983–86, 1989	60
Allen Adkins	Clovis, Calif.	1954–57	14
Mike Alexander	Franklin, Tenn.	1980–81, 1984–85, 1988–90	74
Johnny Allen (1)	**Greenville, S.C.**	**1955–67**	**173**
Loy Allen Jr.	Raleigh, N.C.	1993–97, 1999	48
Bobby Allison (85)	**Hueytown, Ala.**	**1961, 1965–88**	**718**
Davey Allison (19)	**Hueytown, Ala.**	**1985–93**	**191**
Donnie Allison (10)	**Hueytown, Ala.**	**1966–83, 1986, 1988**	**242**
George Alsobrook	Hiram, Ga.	1958–59, 1961–62	18
George Althiede	Morristown, Tenn.	1971–72	16
Bill Amick (1)	**Portland, Ore.**	**1954–57, 1961, 1963–65**	**48**
Jack Anderson	Pearisburg, Pa.	1963–65	36
John Anderson	Massilon, Ohio	1979–83	32
John Andretti (2)	**Bethlehem, Pa.**	**1993–2005**	**340**
Mario Andretti (1)	**Nazareth, Pa.**	**1966–69**	**14**
Bob Apperson	Charlottesville, Va.	1949–50, 1952	11
Ben Arnold	Fairfield, Ala.	1968–73	132
Buddy Arrington	Martinsville, Va.	1964–88	562
Casey Atwood	Antioch, Tenn.	2000–03	75
L.D. Austin	Greenville, S.C.	1957–62	169
Jimmy Ayers	Gardendale, Ala.	1950–55	19

193

B

Don Bailey	Brockway, Pa.	1951, 1956–57	12
H.B. Bailey	Houston, Texas	1964–73, 1975, 1977, 1979, 1981–93	87
Buck Baker (46)	**Charlotte, N.C.**	**1949–73, 1976**	**637**
Buddy Baker (19)	**Charlotte, N.C.**	**1959–92**	**699**
Charlie Baker	New Oxford, Pa.	1982, 1986–90	13
Randy Baker	Charlotte, N.C.	1982, 1984–88, 1991–92, 1996	14
Rick Baldwin	Corpus Christi, Texas	1981–85, 1986	11
Walter Ballard	Houston, Texas	1966, 1971–78	176
Earl Balmer (1)	**Floyds Knob, Ind.**	**1959, 1964–68**	**32**
Gary Balough	Fort Lauderdale, Fla.	1979–82, 1991–92	22
Phil Barkdoll	Phoenix, Ariz.	1984–92	23
Johnny Barnes	Port Charlotte, Fla.	1971, 1973–74	13
Stan Barrett	Bishop, Calif.	1980–82, 1989–90	19
Stanton Barrett	Bishop, Calif.	1999, 2004–present	21
Bob Barron	Bradenton, Fla.	1960–61	32
Larry Baumel	Sparta, Wis.	1969–71	45
Hal Beal	Portland, Ore.	1956–57, 1963	10
Herman Beam	Johnson City, Tenn.	1957–63	194
Dick Beaty	Charlotte, N.C.	1955–58	38
Johnny Beauchamp (2)	**Harlan, Iowa**	**1953, 1957–61**	**23**
Andy Belmont	Langhorne, Pa.	1989, 1991–92, 2004	12
Ed Benedict	Miamisburg, Ohio	1951–53	12
Bill Benson	Far Rockaway, N.J.	1957–58	16
Johnny Benson Jr. (1)	**Grand Rapids, Mich.**	**1996–2005**	**271**
Ed Berrier	Winston-Salem, N.C.	1995–97, 1999–2000	19
Tony Bettenhausen Jr.	Indianapolis, Ind.	1973–74, 1982	33
Rich Bickle	Edgerton, Wis.	1989–95, 1997–2001	85
Don Biederman	Port Credit, Ontario	1967–69	42
Eddie Bierschwale	San Antonio, Texas	1983–92	117
Greg Biffle (10)	**Vancouver, Wash.**	**2002–present**	**141**
Terry Bivins	Shawnee Mission, Kan.	1975–77	28
Gene Black	Arden, N.C.	1965–66, 1968	37
Bunkie Blackburn	Fayetteville, N.C.	1960–66, 1970	71
Bill Blair (3)	**High Point, N.C.**	**1949–58**	**.123**
Dave Blaney	Hartford, Ohio	1992, 1999–present	226
Mike Bliss	Milwaukie, Ore.	1998–2000, 2002–05	71
Jim Blomgren	El Monte, Calif.	1956–64	20
Brett Bodine (1)	**Chemung, N.Y.**	**1986–2003**	**480**
Geoffrey Bodine (18)	**Chemung, N.Y.**	**1979–2004**	**570**
Todd Bodine	Chemung, N.Y.	1992–2005	226
David Ray Boggs	Morrisville, N.C.	1971–73	32

Neil Bonnett (18)	**Bessemer, Ala.**	**1974–90, 1993**	362
Joe Booher	West Lafayette, Ind.	1978, 1980–83, 1985–86, 1988	21
Ken Bouchard	Fitchburg, Mass	1987–89, 1993–94	33
Ron Bouchard (1)	**Fitchburg, Mass.**	**1981–87**	160
Jerry Bowman	Havre D'Grace, Md.	1982–87	19
Chuck Bown	Portland, Ore.	1972–81, 1990–91, 1993–96	73
Dick Bown	Portland, Ore.	1963, 1965, 1969–75	20
Jim Bown	Portland, Ore.	1981–90	23
Clint Bowyer	Emporia, Kan.	2005–06	28
Trevor Boys	Alsa Craig, Ontario	1982–89, 1993	102
Gary Bradberry	Chelsea, Ala.	1994–2000, 2002	47
Jim Bray	Long Beach, Ontario	1962–65, 1974	13
Richard Brickhouse (1)	**Rocky Point, N.C.**	**1968–70, 1979, 1982**	39
Buck Brigance	Charlotte, N.C.	1958–60	16
Dick Brooks (1)	**Porterville, Calif.**	**1969–85**	358
Earl Brooks	Lynchburg, Va.	1962–77, 1979	263
Perk Brown	Spray, N.C.	1952–55, 1964	28
Darrell Bryant	Thomasville, N.C.	1964–66, 1976	18
Herschel Buchanan	Shreveport, La.	1950–54	23
Bob Burcham	Rossville, Ga.	1968–69, 1974–79	37
Bob Burdick (1)	**Omaha, Neb.**	**1959–62**	15
Marvin Burke (1)	**Pittsburg , Calif.**	**1951**	1
Carl Burris	Leaksville, N.C.	1953–54, 1958–60	10
Jeff Burton (17)	**South Boston, Va.**	**1993–present**	430
Ward Burton (5)	**South Boston, Va.**	**1994–2004**	356
Kurt Busch (15)	**Las Vegas, Nev.**	**2000–present**	211
Kyle Busch (3)	**Las Vegas, Nev.**	**2004–present**	69
Red Byron (2)	**Anniston, Ala.**	**1949–51**	15

C

Scotty Cain	Venice, Calif.	1956–61, 1963, 1965–71	36
Wally Campbell	Trenton, N.J.	1949–51, 1953	11
Earle Canavan	Fort Johnson, N.Y.	1969, 1971–79, 1982, 1985–86	70
Jimmy Lee Capps	Jacksonville, Fla.	1964, 1976–78	11
Billy Carden	Mableton, Ga.	1949–59	73
Pancho Carter	Brownsburg, Ill.	1985–86, 1990, 1992, 1994–95	14
Raymond Carter	Henry, Va.	1964–65	10
Neil Castles	Charlotte, N.C.	1957–60, 1962–76	498
Chad Chaffin	Smyrna, Tenn.	2004–present	10
Ted Chamberlain	St. Petersburg, Fla.	1949–55, 1957–59	63
Bill Champion	Norfolk, Va.	1951, 1955–59, 1962, 1965–76	289
Mike Chase	Bakersfield, Calif.	1990–94	13

Richard Childress	Winston-Salem, N.C.	1969, 1971–81	285
Steve Christman	Fort Wayne, Ind.	1987	20
Joe Clark	Neptune Beach, Fla.	1961, 1964–68, 1970–71	14
Gene Cline	Rome, Ga.	1966	13
Ed Cole	Pinehurst, N.C.	1955–57	26
Neil Cole (1)	**Oakland, N.J.**	**1950–53**	**19**
Dean Combs	North Wilkesboro, N.C.	1981–84	24
R.L. Combs	North Wilkesboro, N.C.	1957–59	21
Rodney Combs	Cincinnati, Ohio	1982–84, 1986–90	55
Stacy Compton	Lynchburg, Va.	1996, 1999–2003	88
Gene Comstock	Chesapeake, Ohio	1950–55	29
Jim Cook (1)	**Norwalk, Conn.**	**1954–61, 1963–70**	**39**
Bob Cooper	Gastonia, N.C.	1962–69	64
Doug Cooper	Gastonia, N.C.	1963–68	114
Derrike Cope (2)	**Spanaway, Wash.**	**1982, 1984–present**	**406**
Delma Cowart	Savannah, Ga.	1981–87, 1992	21
Lowell Cowell	Morgantown, W. Va.	1981–83	10
Doug Cox	Greenville, S.C.	1955–61	30
James Cox	Radford, Va.	1969–72	22
Thomas Cox	Asheboro, N.C.	1962–63	44
Jerry Cranmer	Atlantic City, N.J.	1986–87	10
Ricky Craven (2)	**Newburgh, Maine**	**1991, 1995–2004**	**279**
Jimmy Crawford	East Point, Ga.	1970–74	14
Charlie Cregar	Bloomsbury, N.J.	1954–59	16
Curtis Crider	Abbeyville, S.C.	1959–65	232
Pepper Cunningham	Trenton, N.J.	1949–55	11

D

Wally Dallenbach Jr.	Basalt, Colo.	1991–2001	226
Dean Dalton	Asheville, N.C.	1971–77	118
Lloyd Dane (4)	**Eldon, Mo.**	**1951, 1954–61, 1963–64**	**53**
Dan Daughty	Punta Gorda, Fla.	1974–75	10
George Davis	Adelphi, Md.	1967–69	28
Joel Davis	Tenneville, Ga.	1963, 1966–67	30
Jim Delaney	Lyndhurst, N.J.	1949–51, 1957	11
Bill Dennis	Glen Allen, Va.	1962, 1967, 1969–74, 1976, 1978–79, 1981	83
Bob Derrington	Houston, Texas	1964–66	79
Clarence DeZalia	Aberdeen, Md.	1955, 1957–59	58
Darel Dieringer (7)	**Indianapolis, Ind.**	**1957–58, 1961–69, 75**	**181**
C.H. Dingler	Birmingham, Ala.	1951–56	16
Dave Dion	Hudson, N.H.	1978–81, 1983	12
Dick Dixon	Warehouse Point, Conn.	1960, 1962, 1965	11

John Dodd	Glen Burnie, Md.	1953–59	11
Johnny Dodson	King, N.C.	1956–57	15
Mark Donohue (1)	**Newtown Square, Pa.**	**1972–73**	**6**
Fred Dove	Martinsville, Va.	1952–55	47
Jerry Draper	Silvis, Ill.	1953, 1958–59	10
Bob Duell	Warren, Pa.	1956–60	28
Philip Duffie	Augusta, Ga.	1982–83, 1988, 1990	12
Ray Duhigg	Toledo, Ohio	1950–55	54
Gerald Duke	College Park, Ga.	1959–62	17
George Dunn	Raleigh, N.C.	1958–59, 1962	12
Glenn Dunnaway	Gastonia, N.C.	1949–51	19
Clark Dwyer	Littleton, Colo.	1983–85	59

E

Harvey Eakin	Baltimore, Md.	1954–57	17
Dale Earnhardt (76)	**Kannapolis, N.C.**	**1975–2001**	**676**
Dale Earnhardt Jr. (17)	**Kannapolis, N.C.**	**1999–present**	**245**
Ralph Earnhardt	Kannapolis, N.C.	1956–57, 1961–64	51
Sonny Easley	Van Nuys, Calif.	1972–77	19
Carl Edwards (4)	**Columbia, Mo.**	**2004–present**	**76**
Ray Elder (2)	**Carruthers, Ga.**	**1967–78**	**31**
Hoss Ellington	Wilmington, N.C.	1968–70	21
Bill Elliott (44)	**Dawsonville, Ga.**	**1976–present**	**752**
Stick Elliott	Shelby, N.C.	1962–67, 1971	94
Tommy Ellis	Richmond, Va.	1976, 1981–91	94
Bill Elswick	North Miami. Fla.	1979–81	17
George England	Dallas, Texas	1966–68, 1974	10
Erick Erickson	Lancaster, Calif.	1950–56	33
Bill Ervin	Tellico Plains, Tenn.	1967–69	24
Paul Ervin	Bloomfield, N.J.	1951–54	10
Ron Esau	Lakeside, Calif.	1975–76, 1983–90	17
Herbert Estes	Knoxville, Tenn.	1956, 1958	12
Joe Eubanks (1)	**Spartanburg, S.C.**	**1950–61**	**159**

F

Harold Fagan	Willowdale, Ontario	1967–68, 1970–71	20
Red Farmer	Hialeah, Fla.	1953, 1956, 1960, 1962, 1965, 1967–75	36
Bud Farrell	Augusta, Ga.	1951–52	11
Doc Faustina	Las Vegas, Nev.	1971–72, 1975–76	10
Ron Fellows	Toronto, Ontario	1995, 1998, 1999–present	15
Jim Fiebelkorn	Randolph, N.Y.	1951–52	18
Joe Fields	Montpelier, Vt.	1979, 1981–84, 1986	16

Lou Figaro (1)	**Inglewood, Calif.**	**1951, 1954**	**16**
Chet Fillip	San Angelo, Texas	1985–87	24
Ken Fisher	Hamburg, N.Y.	1954–55	14
Christian Fittipaldi	Sao Paulo, Brazil	2002–03	16
Bob Flock (4)	**Atlanta, Ga.**	**1949–52, 1954–55, 1956**	**36**
Fonty Flock (19)	**Decatur, Ga.**	**1949–57**	**154**
Tim Flock (39)	**Atlanta, Ga.**	**1949–61**	**188**
Jimmy Florian (1)	**Cleveland, Ohio**	**1950–52, 1954**	**26**
George Follmer	Acradia, Calif.	1972, 1974–75, 1986–87	20
Red Foote	Southington, Conn.	1962–63, 1965	10
Elliott Forbes-Robinson	LaCresenta, Calif.	1977, 1981–84	22
Bill Foster	High Point, N.C.	1961–63	16
A.J. Foyt (7)	**Houston, Texas**	**1963–90, 1992, 1994**	**128**
Larry Foyt	Houston, Texas	2003–04	23
Larry Frank (1)	**Indianapolis, Ind.**	**1956–66**	**103**
Joe Frasson	Golden Valley, Minn.	1969–79	107
Jeff Fuller	Auburn, Mass.	1992, 2000, 2004–05	13

G

Ernie Gahan	Dover, N.H.	1960–62, 1966	11
Tommy Gale	McKeesport, Pa.	1968–73, 1975–84, 1986	245
Harry Gant (18)	**Taylorsville, N.C.**	**1973–94**	**474**
Johnny Gardner	Rock Hill, S.C.	1958	14
Walson Gardner	Lauringburg, N.C.	1965–69	24
Charles Gattalia	New Haven, Conn.	1951–52	14
Brendan Gaughan	Las Vegas, Nev.	2004	36
Bobby Gerhart	Lebanon, Pa.	1983–90, 1992	24
Dick Getty	Van Nuys, Calif.	1956–57, 1959–62	26
Mickey Gibbs	Glencoe, Ala.	1988–91	36
Wayne Gillette	Atlanta, Ga.	1969	16
Butch Gilliland	Anaheim, Calif.	1990–95, 1997–99	10
Charlie Glotzbach (4)	**Edwardsville, Ind.**	**1960–61, 1967–76, 1981, 1990, 1992**	**123**
Paul Goldsmith (9)	**St. Claire Shores, Mich.**	**1956–58, 1961–64, 1966–69**	**127**
Cecil Gordon	Horse Shoe, N.C.	1968–83, 1985	450
Jeff Gordon (75)	**Vallejo, Calif.**	**1992–2006**	**464**
Robby Gordon (3)	**Cerritos, Calif.**	**1991, 1993, 1994, 1996–98, 2000–present**	**226**
Jerry Grant	Escondido, Calif.	1965–68, 1973–74	19
Danny Graves (1)	**Modesto, Calif.**	**1957–58**	**9**
Eddie Gray (4)	**Gardena, Calif.**	**1957–61, 1963–66**	**22**
Henley Gray	Rome, Ga.	1964–77	373
David Green	Owensboro, Ky.	1997–2000, 2003–04	78
George Green	Johnson City, Tenn.	1956–63	116

Jeff Green	Owensboro, Ky.	1994, 1996–99, 2001–present	223
Charley Griffith	Chattanooga, Tenn.	1958–60, 1962–63	17
Steve Grissom	Gadsden, Ala.	1990, 1993–2000, 2002	151
Dan Gurney (5)	**Costa Mesa, Calif.**	**1962–70, 1980**	**16**
Janet Guthrie	New York, N.Y.	1976–78, 1980	33

H

Royce Haggerty (1)	**Portland, Ore.**	**1955–57**	**9**
Johnny Halford	Spartanburg, S.C.	1969–72, 1978	41
Roy Hallquist	Stratford, Conn.	1962–63, 1966, 1968–69	10
J.V. Hamby	Columbia, S.C.	1958, 1961–62, 1964	13
Roger Hamby	Ferguson, N.C.	1977–81	67
Bobby Hamilton (4)	**Nashville, Tenn.**	**1989–2002, 2005**	**371**
Bobby Hamilton Jr.	Mount Juliet, Tenn.	2000–05	64
Pete Hamilton (4)	**Dedham, Mass.**	**1968–73**	**64**
Denny Hamlin (2)	**Midlothian, Va.**	**2005–present**	**34**
Mack Hanbury	Hyattsville, Md.	1955–56	10
Chuck Hansen	Whiteford, Md.	1954–58	26
Fred Harb	High Point, N.C.	1955–65	144
Jack Harden	Huntsville, Ala.	1967	10
Harold Hardesty	Pasco, Wash.	1956–58, 1968–69	16
Bud Harless	Gilber, W. Va.	1953–55, 1963–65	28
Ferrel Harris	Pikeville, N.Y.	1975–80, 1982	41
Bill Harrison	Topeka, Kansas	1949–51, 1953–55	10
Butch Hartman	Zanesville, Ohio	1966, 1968, 1972, 1977–79	20
Kevin Harvick (9)	**Bakersfield, Calif.**	**2001–present**	**205**
Friday Hassler	Chattanooga, Tenn.	1960–62, 1966–72	135
Bob Havenmann	Eureka, Calif.	1954–58	11
Pete Hazelwood	Cartersville, Ga.	1969–70	19
Harvey Hege	Thomasville, N.C.	1958–61	25
Jimmy Helms	Charlotte, N.C.	1964–67	88
Elmo Henderson	Spartanburg, S.C.	1959–61, 1964–65	21
Harvey Henderson	Beltsville, Md.	1952, 1955–58, 1961	40
Ray Hendrick	Richmond, Va.	1956, 1962–63, 1967–69, 1971–74	17
Jimmy Hensley	Ridgeway, Va.	1972–77, 1981–82, 1984, 1986, 1988, 1990–95	98
Russ Hepler	Clairon, Pa.	1951–52, 1954, 57	13
Ben Hess	Dayton, Ohio	1988–90, 1995	12
Larry Hess	Oil City, Pa.	1965–69	27
Ed Hessert	Trenton, N.J.	1969–72	22
Doug Heveron	Liverpool, N.Y.	1984–86	31
Elton Hildreth	Bridgeton, N.J.	1952–57	51
Bruce Hill	Topeka, Kansas	1974–81	100

Andy Hillenburg	Indianapolis, Ind.	1991, 1993, 1995, 1998–99, 2002, 2004	16
Bobby Hillin Jr. (1)	**Midland, Texas**	**1982–97, 2000**	**334**
Gene Hobby	Henderson, N.C.	1964–66	35
Al Holbert	Warrington, Pa.	1976, 1978–79	19
Bill Hollar	Burlington, N.C.	1970–73, 1975–76, 1978–80	29
Paul Dean Holt	Sweetwater, Tenn.	1966–69, 1975, 1977	85
Ron Hornaday	San Fernando, Calif.	1955, 1957–61, 1963, 1966, 1971, 1973	17
Ron Hornaday Jr.	Palmdale, Calif.	1992–95, 98–2003	45
Jimmy Horton	Folsom, N.J.	1987–90, 1992–95	48
Pappy Hough	Paterson, N.J.	1950–52, 1955	21
Andy Houston	Hickory, N.C.	2000–01	22
Tommy Houston	Hickory, N.C.	1980–82, 1985	13
Chuck Huckabee	Chattanooga, Tenn.	1963–64	12
Don Hume	Belvedere, N.J.	1964–65, 1981, 1984–85	15
T.C. Hunt	Atlanta, Ga.	1960–63, 1965, 1969	24
Mark Hurley	Mahoment, Ill.	1961–64	16
Jim Hurtubise (1)	**N. Tonawanda, N.Y.**	**1957, 1963–64, 1966–72, 1974, 1976–77**	**36**
Dick Hutcherson (14)	**Keokuk, Iowa**	**1964–67**	**103**
Sonny Hutchins	Richmond, Va.	1955, 1965–70, 1973–74	38
James Hylton (2)	**Inman, S.C.**	**1964, 1966–83, 1985–87, 1989–93**	**601**

I

Jack Ingram	Asheville, N.C.	1965–68, 1979, 1981	19
Jimmy Insolo	Mission Hills, Calif.	1970–79, 1981–83	28
Ernie Irvan (15)	**Modesto, Calif.**	**1987–99**	**313**
Kenny Irwin Jr.	Indianapolis, Ind.	1997–2000	87
Tommy Irwin	Keyesville, Va.	1958–63	099
Bobby Isaac (37)	**Catawba, N.C.**	**1961, 1963–76**	**308**

J

Bruce Jacobi	Indianapolis, Ind.	1975–76, 1980–81	20
Bob James	Cuyahoga Falls, Ohio	1951, 1963	11
Dale Jarrett (32)	**Hickory, N.C.**	**1984, 1986–present**	**630**
Glenn Jarrett	Conover, N.C.	1978–83	10
Ned Jarrett (50)	**Newton, N.C.**	**1953–66**	**353**
Harry Jefferson	Naches, Wash.	1973–77	12
Gordon Johncock	Coldwater, Mich.	1966–67, 1972–73, 1975	21
Bobby Johns (2)	**Miami, Fla.**	**1956–69**	**141**
Dick Johnson	Elverta, Calif.	1967–69	56
Jimmie Johnson (22)	**El Cajon, Calif.**	**2001–present**	**174**
Joe Lee Johnson (2)	**Chattanooga, Tenn.**	**1957–62**	**.55**
Junior Johnson (50)	**Ronda, N.C.**	**1953–66**	**313**

Ken Johnson	Jamestown, N.Y.	1956, 1958–61	12
Lionel Johnson	Unionville, Va.	1965–66	15
Slick Johnson	Florence, S.C.	1979–85, 1987	68
Carl Joiner	Portland, Ore.	1957, 1961, 1963, 1966, 1968, 1970–77	16
Alton Jones	Pleasant Grove, Ala.	1970, 1973–75	13
Buckshot Jones	Norcross, Ga.	1997–2003	56
Joe Jones	Winston-Salem, N.C.	1961–63	12
P.J. Jones	Rolling Hills, Calif.	1993–94, 2000, 2003–present	22
Parnelli Jones (4)	**Torrance, Calif.**	**1956–60, 1963–65, 1967–70**	**34**
Lewi Jones	Mango, Fla.	1952, 1955–60, 1963–65	47
Ralph Jones	Upton, Ky.	1977–80, 1988	20
Dick Joslin	Orlando, Fla.	1955, 1957–60	10

K

Reds Kagle	Greenbelt, Md.	1954, 1956–59, 1961	25
Kasey Kahne (6)	**Enumclaw, Wash.**	**2004–present**	**99**
Iggy Katona	Willis, Mich.	1951–52, 1965–66, 1974	13
Bobby Keck	Graham, N.C.	1956–59, 1963–64	98
Bob Keefe	Yakima, Wash.	1956–59	13
Al Keller (2)	**Buffalo, N.Y.**	**1949–50, 1952–54, 1956**	**29**
Tommy Kendall	LeCanada, Calif.	1987–94, 1996, 1998	14
John Kennedy	Villa Park, Ill.	1969, 1977–79	20
John Kenney	Poquoson, Va.	1969–70	12
Matt Kenseth (14)	**Cambridge, Wis.**	**1998–present**	**247**
Ron Keselowski	Troy, Mich.	1970–74	68
John Kieper (1)	**Portland, Ore.**	**1954–57, 1975–77**	**16**
Brownie King	Johnson City, Tenn.	1956–61	97
Bub King	Corbin, Ky.	1950–54	35
Harold Kite (1)	**East Point, Ga.**	**1950–51, 1955–56, 1965**	**9**
Mike Klapak	Warren, Ohio	1950–53	12
Ronnie Kohler	Patterson, N.J	1951–54	13
John Krebs	Roseville, Calif.	1982–94	19
Alan Kulwicki (5)	**Greenfield, Wis.**	**1985–93**	**207**
Travis Kvapil	Janesville, Wis.	2004–present	62

L

Bobby Labonte (21)	**Corpus Christi, Texas**	**1991, 1993–present**	**465**
Terry Labonte (22)	**Corpus Christi, Texas**	**1978–present**	**845**
Randy LaJoie	Norwalk, Conn.	1985–86, 1988–91, 1994–95, 1998–99, 2004–05	44
Sonny Lamphear	Charlotte, N.C.	1966	13
Shep Langdon	Angier, N.C.	1957–60	45
Elmo Langley (2)	**Landover, Md.**	**1954–79, 1981**	**538**

Mel Larson	Phoenix, Ariz.	1955–60, 1970, 1972–73, 1975, 1978	47
Coleman Lawrence	Martinsville, Va.	1951–53	22
Harry Leake	Lewisville, N.C.	1958, 1961–62	22
Max Ledbetter	Franklin, N.C.	1966–69	21
Jason Leffler	Indianapolis, Ind.	2001–05	62
Kevin Lepage	Shelburne, Vt.	1997–present	196
Danny Letner (2)	**Downey, Calif.**	**1951, 1954–57, 1959, 1961, 1963**	**27**
Jimmie Lewallen	Archdale, N.C.	1949–60	142
Paul Lewis (1)	**Johnson City, Tenn.**	**1960–68**	**114**
Ralph Liguori	Bronx, N.Y.	1951–56	76
Dick Linder (3)	**Pittsburgh, Pa.**	**1949–51, 1953, 1956**	**28**
Butch Lindley	Greenville, S.C.	1979, 1981–83, 1985	11
John Lindsay	Jersey City, N.J.	1954–56, 1958	15
Chad Little	Spokane, Wash.	1986–2000, 2002	217
Ed Livingston	Folly Beach, S.C.	1961–64	47
Carl Long	Roxboro, N.C.	2000–02, 2004–present	23
Fred Lorenzen (26)	**Elmhurst, Ill.**	**1956, 1960–67, 1970–72**	**158**
Clarence Lovell	San Antonio, Texas	1972–73	16
DeWayne Lund (5)	**Cross, S.C.**	**1955–73, 1975**	**.303**
Clyde Lynn	Christiansburg, Va.	1965–71, 1976	165

M

Johnny Mackison	Delta, Pa.	1957–58	16
Dave Mader III	Maylene, Ala.	1989–92	10
Jocko Maggiacomo	Poughkeepsie, N.Y.	1977–83, 1986–88	23
Chuck Mahoney	Rome, N.Y.	1949–52, 1956	16
Larry Manning	Salisbury, N.C.	1963–68, 1970, 1974	70
Skip Manning	Bogalusa, La.	1975–79	79
Johnny Mantz (1)	**Long Beach, Calif.**	**1950–51, 1955–56**	**12**
Dave Marcis (5)	**Wausau, Wis.**	**1968–2002**	**883**
Coo Coo Marlin	Columbia, Tenn.	1966–67, 1968–80	165
Sterling Marlin (10)	**Columbia, Tenn.**	**1976, 1977–present**	**702**
Mark Martin (35)	**Batesville, Ark.**	**1981–83, 1986–present**	**666**
Otis Martin	Bassett, Va.	1949–54	23
Jimmy Massey	Birmingham, Ala.	1951, 1953–54, 1956	41
Rick Mast	Rockbridge Baths, Va.	1988–2002	364
Banjo Matthews	Asheville, N.C.	1952, 1955–63	51
Nace Mattingly	Leonardtown, Md.	1955–60, 1963	17
Bobby Mausgrover	Keokuk, Iowa	1967–73	46
Dick May	Watertown, N.Y.	1970–85	186
Jeremy Mayfield (5)	**Owensboro, Ky.**	**1993–present**	**402**
Roy Mayne	Sumter, S.C.	1963–74	139

Jack McCoy	Bakersfield, Calif.	1963, 1966–74	20
Rick McCray	Bloomington, Calif.	1978–89	25
J.D. McDuffie	Sanford, N.C.	1963, 1966–91	653
John McFadden	Forest City, N.C.	1982–83, 1989, 1992	11
John McGinley	Chicora, Pa.	1951, 1954–55	11
Pop McGinnis	Huntington, W. Va.	1952–55, 1964, 1970	22
Hershel McGriff (4)	**Bridal Veil, Ore.**	**1950–54, 1971–78, 1980–93**	**87**
Bill McMahan	Dandridge, Tenn.	1964–65	21
Worth McMillion	Amelia, Va.	1962–69	62
Jamie McMurray (1)	**Joplin, Mo.**	**2002–present**	**141**
Sam McQuagg (1)	**Columbus, Ga.**	**1962, 1964–69, 1974**	**62**
John McVitty	Mamaroneck, N.Y.	1955–56	11
Jimmy Means	Huntsville, Ala.	1976–93	455
Casey Mears	Bakersfield, Calif.	2003–present	135
Chuck Meekins	Los Angeles, Calif.	1951, 1954–57	24
Ken Meisenhelder	Springfield, Mass.	1968–71	51
Major Melton	Laurinburg, N.C.	1963–64	20
Stan Meserve	Winslow, Maine	1968	31
Joe Mihalic	Pittsburgh, Pa.	1974–78	38
Butch Miller	Medallion, Ohio	1986–90, 1994	41
Harold Miller	Emerson, Ga.	1975–77	11
Junior Miller	Winston-Salem, N.C.	1976–81	27
Larry Miller	Taylors, S.C.	1967	15
Joe Millikan	Randleman, N.C.	1974, 1979–84, 1986	80
Joel Million	Richmond, Ky.	1954–56	18
Clyde Minter	Martinsville, Va.	1949–55	42
Ralph Moody (5)	**Taunton, Mass.**	**1956–57, 1959, 1962**	**47**
Tommy Moon	Jacksonville, Fla.	1951–54	10
Bud Moore	Charleston, S.C.	1964–68, 1973	31
Bunk Moore	Indian Trail, N.C.	1955–56, 1958–61, 1966	24
Doug Moore	Chattaonooga, Tenn.	1964–65	29
Lloyd Moore (1)	**Frewsburg, N.Y.**	**1949–52, 1955**	**49**
Steve Moore	Carrollton, Ga.	1977–80, 1982–84, 1988	18
Rob Moroso	Madison, Conn.	1988–90	29
Bill Morton	Church Hill, Tenn.	1955, 1957–59, 1961–63, 1965	35
Earl Moss	Creedmoor, N.C.	1951–53, 1956, 1959	11
Arden Mounts	Gilbert, W. Va.	1953–56	37
Frank Mundy (3)	**Atlanta, Ga.**	**1949–52, 1956**	**52**
Ted Musgrave	Franklin, Wis.	1990–2003	305
Billy Myers (2)	**Germanton, N.C.**	**1951–52, 1955–58**	**84**
Bobby Myers	Winston-Salem, N.C.	1951–53, 1956–57	15
Gary Myers	Walnut Cove, N.C.	1974, 1976–77, 1978	46

N

Jerry Nadeau (1)	**Danbury, Conn.**	**1997–2003**	**177**
Ed Negre	Kelso, Wash.	1955–57, 1961, 1967–79	339
Norm Nelson (1)	**Racine, Wis.**	**1955, 1966–68**	**5**
Joe Nemechek (4)	**Naples, Fla.**	**1993–present**	**421**
Ryan Newman (12)	**South Bend, Ind.**	**2000–present**	**179**
Rick Newsom	Fort Mill, S.C.	1972–86	83
Don Noel	Arletto, Calif.	1960–61, 1963–64, 1967–73, 1977–79	24
Brad Noffsinger	Huntington Beach, Calif.	1988	17
G.T. Nolan	Jetersville, Va.	1965–68	13
Whitey Norman	Winston-Salem, N.C.	1956–59	29
Bill Norton (1)	**Gardena, Calif.**	**1951, 1953**	**4**

O

Joe Bill O'Dell	Baltimore, Md.	1953–54, 1956–57	11
Randy Ogden	Woodward, Okla.	1979–81	10
Dan Oldenberg	Highland, Ind.	1951–57	20
Jerry O'Neil	Auburn, N.Y.	1989–90, 1992–93	16
Bill Osborne	Rialto, Calif.	1971–72, 1974–75, 1977, 1980, 1985–86	13
Nelson Oswald	Jamestown, N.C.	1978–80	14
L.D. Ottinger	Newport, Tenn.	1966, 1973–74, 1984	10
Cotton Owens (9)	**Spartanburg, S.C.**	**1950–64**	**160**

P

Eddie Pagan (4)	**Lynwood, Calif.**	**1954–59, 1961–63**	**62**
Lenny Page	Buffalo, N.Y.	1956–57, 1959–60	12
Clyde Palmer	Monte Vista, Calif.	1954–57, 1961	22
Marvin Panch (17)	**Oakland, Calif.**	**1951, 1953–66**	**216**
Richie Panch	Daytona Beach, Fla.	1973–76	47
Jimmy Pardue (2)	**North Wilkesboro, N.C.**	**1955–56, 1959–64**	**217**
Steve Park (2)	**East Northport, N.Y.**	**1997–2003**	**181**
Paul Parks	Columbus, Ohio	1950–51, 1953, 1960–61	13
George Parrish	Henderson, N.C.	1954–55, 1957–58	21
Jim Parsley	Wheaton, N.D.	1958–59	11
Benny Parsons (21)	**Ellerbe, N.C.**	**1964, 1969–88**	**526**
Phil Parsons (1)	**Denver, N.C.**	**1983–89, 1990, 1992–95, 1997**	**203**
Vic Parsons	Willowdale, Ontario	1972–73	19
Jim Paschal (25)	**High Point, N.C.**	**1949–68, 1970–72**	**422**
Ed Paskovich	Hackensack, N.J.	1953–55	10
Dick Passwater (1)	**Indianapolis, Ind.**	**1952–53**	**20**
Johnny Patterson	Huntington, W. Va.	1952–56, 1959	25
David Pearson (105)	**Spartanburg, S.C.**	**1960–86**	**574**

Larry Pearson	Spartanburg, S.C.	1986–91	57
Peck Peckham	Old Bridge, N.J.	1954–58	27
Jack Pennington	Augusta, Ga.	1989–90	16
Bob Perry	Hawthorne, Calif.	1957–61, 1963	18
Paul Pettit	Danbury, Conn.	1950–54, 1955	12
Kyle Petty (8)	**Randleman, N.C.**	**1979–present**	**776**
Lee Petty (54)	**Randleman, N.C.**	**1949–64**	**427**
Maurice Petty	Randleman, N.C.	1960–64	26
Richard Petty (200)	**Randleman, N.C.**	**1958–1992**	**1,184**
Howard Phillippi	Torrance, Calif.	1954–58	11
Tom Pistone (2)	**Chicago, Ill.**	**1955–57, 1959–62, 1965–68**	**130**
Blackie Pitt	Rocky Mount, N.C.	1954–56, 1958	81
Dick Poling	Sumter, S.C.	1969, 1971	15
Lennie Pond (1)	**Ettrick, Va.**	**1969–70, 1973–85, 1988–89**	**235**
Bill Poor	Wheaton, Mo.	1956–59	31
Marvin Porter (2)	**Lakewood, Calif.**	**1957–61, 1963–64, 1967**	**34**
Mike Potter	Johnson City, Tenn.	1979–90, 1992–93	59
George Poulos	Charlotte, N.C.	1967	23
Robert Pressley	Asheville, N.C.	1994–2002	205
Baxter Price	Monroe, N.C.	1974–81	90
Scott Pruett	Roseville, Calif.	2000–present	39
Jeff Purvis	Clarksville, Tenn.	1990–97, 2001	50
Don Puskarich	Garden Grove, Calif.	1975–82	17
J.T. Putney	Arden, N.C.	1964–67	125

R

Billy Rafter	Clarence Center, N.Y.	1949, 1953–58	35
Ken Ragan	Unadilla, Ga.	1983–90	50
Tony Raines	LaPorte, Ind.	2002–06	74
Benny Rakestraw	Dallas, Ga.	1956, 1958–59	13
Wilbur Rakestraw	Dallas, Ga.	1956, 1958–61	30
Dick Rathman (13)	**Los Angeles, Calif.**	**1951–55**	**128**
Jim Reed (7)	**Peekskill, N.Y.**	**1951–63**	**106**
Lee Reitzel	Charlotte, N.C.	1961–63	29
Bill Rexford (1)	**Conowango Valley, N.C.**	**1949–53**	**36**
Jack Reynolds	Hawthorne, N.J.	1950–52	14
Harlan Richardson	Houston, Texas	1959, 1961–62	15
Tim Richmond (13)	**Ashland, Ohio**	**1980–87**	**185**
Jody Ridley (1)	**Chatsworth, Ga.**	**1973–77, 1979–84, 1986**	**140**
Scott Riggs	Bahama, N.C.	2004–present	97
Bob Riley	Norwalk, Conn.	1980–81, 1983–85	10
Richard Riley	Charlotte, N.C.	1956, 1959–60	15

Marty Robbins	Glendale, Ariz.	1966, 1968, 1970–75, 1977–80, 1982	35
Charlie Roberts	Anniston, Ala.	1971–74	73
Glenn Roberts (33)	**Daytona Beach, Fla.**	**1950–64**	**207**
Johnny Roberts	Brooklyn, Md.	1953–56, 1961	13
Jim Robinson	North Hollywood, Calif.	1979–87	21
Jackie Rogers	Wilmington, N.C.	1974–76	50
Shorty Rollins (1)	**Corpus Christi, Texas**	**1958–60**	**43**
Jim Roper (1)	**Halstead, Kan.**	**1949**	**2**
Bob Ross	Lakewood, Calif.	1956–61, 1963	17
Earl Ross (1)	**Alsa Craig, Ontario**	**1973–76**	**26**
John Rostek (1)	**Fort Collins, Colo.**	**1960, 1963**	**6**
Ricky Rudd (23)	**Chesapeake, Va.**	**1975–2005**	**875**
Ken Rush	High Point, N.C.	1957–59, 1961–64, 1971–72	56
Johnny Rutherford (1)	**Fort Worth, Texas**	**1963–66, 1972–77, 1981, 1988**	**35**
Joe Ruttman	Upland, Calif.	1963–64, 1977, 1980–95	218
Terry Ryan	Davenport, Iowa	1976–77	12

S

Greg Sacks (1)	**Mattituck, N.Y.**	**1983–98, 2004–05**	**263**
Elliott Sadler (3)	**Emporia, Va.**	**1998–present**	**270**
Hermie Sadler	Emporia, Va.	1996, 2001–present	59
Bucky Sager	Toledo, Ohio	1950–52, 1954	16
Boris Said	Carlsbad, Calif.	1999–present	25
Gary Sain	Hickory, N.C.	1962–63, 1967	16
Leon Sales (1)	**Winston-Salem, N.C.**	**1950–52**	**8**
Ed Samples	Atlanta, Ga.	1951–52, 1954	12
Marshall Sargent	Salinas, Calif.	1957–64	12
Jim Sauter	Necedah, Wis.	1980, 1982–93, 1996	77
Elton Sawyer	Chesapeake, Va.	1995–96	29
Lucky Sawyer	Baltimore, Md.	1953–53, 1956–57	10
Connie Saylor	Johnson City, Tenn.	1978–88	57
Bob Schacht	Lombard, Ill.	1981–82, 1988–89, 1992–94	25
Bill Schmitt	Redding, Calif.	1975–93	44
Frankie Schneider (1)	**Lambertville, N.J.**	**1949–53, 1957–58**	**27**
Ken Schrader (4)	**Fenton, Mo.**	**1984–present**	**695**
Volney Schulze	Silver Spring, Md.	1954–58	17
Lyle Scott	Port Washington, N.Y.	1950–51, 1953, 1956	10
Tighe Scott	Pen Argyle, Pa.	1976–80, 1982	89
Wendell Scott (1)	**Danville, Va.**	**1961–73**	**.495**
John Sears	Ellerbe, N.C.	1964–73	318
Bill Sedgwick	Granada Hills, Calif.	1989–93	10
George Seeger	Whittier, Calif.	1951, 1954, 1956–57	19

Bill Seifert	Skyland, N.C.	1966–72, 1977, 1979	235
Ned Setzer	Claremont, N.C.	1965–66	10
Kirk Shelmerdine	Philadelphia, Pa.	1981, 1994, 2002, 2004–present	26
Morgan Shepherd (4)	**Conover, N.C.**	**1970, 1977–78, 1981–2005**	**513**
Bill Shirey	Detroit, Mich.	1969–72	72
Barney Shore	Lewisville, N.C.	1958–60	19
Buddy Shuman (1)	**Charlotte, N.C.**	**1951–53, 1955**	**29**
David Simko	Clarkston, Mich.	1982–84, 1986–88	10
Dub Simpson	Charlotte, N.C.	1967–72, 1974	48
Gene Simpson	Meadville, Pa.	1955–56	23
David Sisco	Nashville, Tenn.	1971–88	133
Dick Skillen	Claremont, Tenn.	1974–77, 1980, 1983, 1985	17
Eddie Skinner	Yerrington, Nev.	1953–58	73
Mike Skinner	Ontario, Calif.	1986, 1990–94, 1996–present	242
Gordon Smith	Enfield, N.C.	1955	15
Jack Smith (21)	**Sandy Springs, Ga.**	**1949–52, 1954–64**	**262**
Larry Smith	Lenoir, N.C.	1971–73	38
Louise Smith	Greenville, S.C.	1949–50, 1952	11
Roy Smith	Victoria, B.C. (Canada)	1975–84, 1987–89	26
Slick Smith	Atlanta, Ga.	1949–55	50
Stanley Smith	Chelsea, Ala.	1990–93	28
Wayne Smith	Advance, N.C.	1965–72	122
Bill Snowden	St. Augustine, Fla.	1949–52	24
John Soares (1)	**Oakland, Calif.**	**1951, 1954–55**	**12**
John Soares Jr.	Hayward, Calif.	1970–73, 1975–76	13
Reed Sorenson	Peachtree City, Ga.	2005–present	29
Sam Sommers	Savannah, Ga.	1976–78	30
David Sosebee	Dawsonville, Ga.	1979, 1986–88	10
Gober Sosebee (2)	**Atlanta, Ga.**	**1949–55, 1958–59**	**.71**
Lake Speed (1)	**Jackson, Miss.**	**1980–98**	**402**
G.C. Spencer	Jonesboro, Tenn.	1958–77	415
Jimmy Spencer (2)	**Berwick, Pa.**	**1989–present**	**478**
Junior Spencer	Hamlin, W. Va.	1964–65, 1971	25
Ken Spikes	Cordele, Ga.	1964, 1967, 1970	16
Nelson Stacy (4)	**Cincinnati, Ohio**	**1952, 1961–65**	**45**
Mark Stahl	San Diego, Calif.	1981–91	30
Gwyn Staley (3)	**Burlington, N.C.**	**1951–58**	**69**
Bill Stammer	Pasadena, Calif.	1951, 1954–56	10
Billy Standridge	Shelby, N.C.	1994–98	23
Johnny Steele	Carmichael, Calif.	1965–69, 1971	11
Chuck Stevenson (1)	**Sidney, Mont.**	**1955–56**	**2**
Pete Stewart	Statesville, N.C.	1953–54, 1956–57, 1963–65	17

Tony Stewart (26)	**Columbus, Ind.**	**1999–present**	**275**
Ramo Stott	Keokuk, Iowa	1967, 1969–77	36
David Stremme	South Bend, Ind.	2005–present	29
Bub Strickler	Timberville, Va.	1965–66, 1970–71, 1979–8	21
Hut Stricklin	Calera, Ala.	1987, 1989–2002	328

T

Don Tarr	Miami Beach, Fla.	1967–71	48
Jesse James Taylor	Macon, Ga.	1950–51, 1956, 1958, 1961	16
Brad Teague	Johnson City, Tenn.	1982, 1986–89, 1991–94	44
Marshall Teague (7)	**Daytona Beach, Fla.**	**1949–52**	**23**
Dave Terrell	Newton, Pa.	1952, 1954–58	68
Kevin Terris	Hermosa Beach, Calif.	1970–72, 1984	11
Donald Thomas (1)	**Olivia, N.C.**	**1950–56**	**79**
Hank Thomas	Winston-Salem, N.C.	1963, 1966	15
Herb Thomas (48)	**Olivia, N.C.**	**1949–57, 1962**	**229**
Jabe Thomas	Christianburg, Va.	1965–76, 1978	322
Larry Thomas	Thomasville, N.C.	1961–64	126
Ronnie Thomas	Christianburg, Va.	1977–89	197
Jimmy Thompson	Monroe, N.C.	1949–52, 1954–55, 1957–62	46
Roscoe Thompson	Forrest Park, Ga.	1950–53, 1958–62	29
Speedy Thompson (20)	**Monroe, N.C.**	**1950–62, 1971**	**198**
Tommy Thompson (1)	**Louisville, Ky.**	**1950–56, 1959**	**22**
Travis Tiller	Triangle, Va.	1974–77, 1979–83	51
Herb Tillman	Miami, Fla.	1953, 1960–62	17
Leonard Tippett	Greenville, S.C.	1951–52	13
Randy Tissot	Hollywood, Fla.	1973–75	13
T.A. Toomes	Asheboro, N.C.	1957	11
Sal Tovella	Chicago, Ill.	1956, 1960–64	14
Dick Trickle	Wisconsin Rapids, Wis.	1970, 1973–78, 1984–86, 1989–2002	303
E.J. Trivette	Deep Gap, N.C.	1959–71	177
Maynard Troyer	Spencerport, N.Y.	1971, 1973	14
Russ Truelove	Waterbury, Conn.	1953, 1955–57	13
Martin Truex Jr.	Mayetta, N.J.	2004–present	36
Curtis Turner (17)	**Roanoke, Va.**	**1949–61, 1965–68**	**184**
Paul Tyler	Palo Alto, Calif.	1971–73	20
Roy Tyner	Red Springs, N.C.	1957–61, 1963–70	311

U

D.K. Ulrich	Woodbury, N.J.	1971–87, 1990, 1992	272
John Utsman	Bluff City, Tenn.	1973, 1976, 1978–80	14
Sherman Utsman	Bluff City, Tenn.	1956, 1961–63	21

V

Bill Vanderhoff	Roseland, N.J.	1967–68	12
Jim Vandiver	Huntersville, N.C.	1968–80, 1983	85
Brian Vickers	Thomasville, N.C.	2003–present	104

W

Bobby Waddell	North Wilkesboro, N.C.	1955–57, 1959–62	37
Billy Wade (4)	**Houston, Texas**	**1962–64**	**71**
Chuck Wahl	Burbank, Calif.	1973–78, 1980	13
Bob Walden	High Point, N.C.	1953, 1958	18
Kenny Wallace	St. Louis, Mo.	1990–91, 1993–present	322
Mike Wallace	St. Louis, Mo.	1991–present	183
Rusty Wallace (55)	**St. Louis, Mo.**	**1980–82, 1984–2005**	**706**
Darrell Waltrip (84)	**Franklin, Tenn.**	**1972–2000**	**809**
Michael Waltrip (4)	**Owensboro, Ky.**	**1985–present**	**667**
Blackie Wangerin	Bloomington, Minn.	1971, 1977–84	27
Frank Warren	Augusta, Ga.	1963–80	396
Gayle Warren	Marion, Va.	1950–51, 1953	15
Al Watkins	Gardendale, Ala.	1954–56	18
Art Watts (1)	**Portland, Ore.**	**1954, 1956–58, 1960–61, 1963**	**19**
Bobby Wawak	Villa Park, Ill.	1965, 1967, 1969, 1971, 1976–87	140
Joe Weatherly (25)	**Norfolk, Va.**	**1952, 1954–64**	**230**
Ewell Weddell	Winston-Salem, N.C.	1950–53	17
Danny Weinberg (1)	**Downey, Calif.**	**1951, 1958–61, 1963–64**	**17**
Bob Welborn (9)	**Denton, N.C.**	**1952–64**	**183**
Al White	Buffalo, N.Y.	1956–60, 1962–66	36
Don White	Keokuk, Iowa	1954–55, 1964, 1966–70, 1972	24
Gene White	Marietta, Ga.	1956, 1958–51	23
Jack White (1)	**Lockport, N.Y.**	**1949–51**	**12**
Rex White (28)	**Spartanburg, S.C.**	**1956–64**	**233**
Richard White	Escondido, Calif.	1973–75, 1977–79	12
Bill Whitley	Winston-Salem, N.C.	1960–64	11
Don Whittington	Lubbock, Texas	1980–81	10
Reb Wickersham	Long Boat Key, Fla.	1960–65	41
Bill Widenhouse	Midland, N.C.	1950–56, 1963–64	31
Dink Widenhouse	Concord, N.C.	1954–56	28
Raymond Williams	Chapel Hill, N.C.	1970–73, 1977–78	93
Fritz Wilson	Denver, Colo.	1959–60, 1965	12
Rick Wilson	Bartow, Fla.	1980–83, 1985–93, 1997	206
Woodie Wilson	Mobile, Ala.	1949, 1955, 1961–62	10
Scott Wimmer	Wausau, Wis.	2000, 2002–present	103
Andy Winfree	Greensboro, N.C.	1953–54	10

Roland Wlodyka	Boston, Mass.	1977–78	11
Glen Wood (4)	**Stuart, Va.**	**1953–61, 1963–64**	**62**
Buzz Woodward	Coatesville, Pa.	1956–59, 1961	13
Bruce Worrell	Lakewood, Calif.	1960–61, 1963–67	12
Johnny Wynn	Grand Rapids, Mich.	1966	21

Y

Eddie Yarboro	Elkin, N.C.	1966–68, 1970–73	33
Cale Yarborough (83)	**Timmonsville, S.C.**	**1957, 1959–88**	**561**
LeeRoy Yarbrough (14)	**Jacksonville, Fla.**	**1960, 1962–72**	**198**
Doug Yates	Chapel Hill, N.C.	1952, 1956, 1958, 1960–62, 1964–65	87
J.J. Yeley	Phoenix, Ariz.	2004–present	33
Shorty York	Mocksville, N.C.	1950–51, 1956–60	12
Buddy Young	Fairfax, Va.	1969–70	23
Ernie Young	Lakewood, Calif.	1954–58	14

Z

Emanuel Zervakis (4)	**Richmond, Va.**	**1956–58, 1960–63**	**83**